Tapestries of Thought

Maureen & Ray

with love

Marilyn

x

Tapestries
of
Thought

Marilyn Holman

Matador
9 Priory Business Park,
Wistow Road, Kibworth Beauchamp,
Leicestershire. LE8 0RX
Tel: 0116 279 2299
Email: books@troubador.co.uk
Web: www.troubador.co.uk/matador
Twitter: @matadorbooks

ISBN 978 1788033 701

British Library Cataloguing in Publication Data.
A catalogue record for this book is available from the British Library.

Printed and bound by CPI Group (UK) Ltd, Croydon, CR0 4YY
Typeset in 10.5pt Aldine by Troubador Publishing Ltd, Leicester, UK

Matador is an imprint of Troubador Publishing Ltd

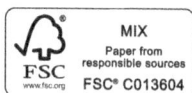

MIX
Paper from
responsible sources
FSC® C013604

To 'Don', my inspiration, my life, my love

Contents

The Tree

Consider the tree, a majestic creation her branches
    outstretched to the world
She knows nothing of taxes or even inflation, just berries
    and green leaves unfurled-
She is home to hundreds of tiny mites from birds and
    rabbits akin
Brave insects to rest on her bark do alight as they travel on
    silky wing-
Many a Stranger has lain here beneath just when the hot
    sun came
She grumbles not when young boys with knives cut into
    her tender frame-
She asks not for much just a space to grow and wildlife for
    company
And in return she will stand and protect from here to
    eternity…

The Moon

Oh palest moon looking down on me-
An innermost troubled soul that you see-
Your special comfort on me bestow-
and ease the sad mind of this daughter below-
Your pale light to calm me and show me the way-
to the peace and tranquillity your soft beams convey-
Oh still languid sphere come to lighten my dreams-
and gather me softly within your pale beams-
Then i shall sleep the great sleep like the stars up above-
and smile down on this place as i leave it my love…

The Morning

Have you ever seen the morning? I mean at very first light
   when a brand new day is breaking through the shadows
   of the night
There are a few stars still about up there in the blue, and
   then the first bird starts to
sing soon others join in too-
As the sun rises higher on his journey overhead see the
   animals of the night scurry
back to find their bed

Such scents there are in the morning such freshness
   everywhere the dew on the grass
that sparkles these things you too can share-
You do not have far to travel to see this revelation-just
   open up your window on the
marvel of creation

The Foster Child

A sad existence a child alone-
No Father or Mother to call my own-
No toys or pets are mine to share-
No welcoming smile for me anywhere-
One day perhaps I will belong-
to somebody somewhere I will grow strong-
In mind and body I will be secure-
Hopeless and lonely will be no more-
I'll find someone and to them I'll cling-
I'll have no need of a wedding ring to keep me there I
    shall be content-
with my own things around me that's how its meant-
to be part of something that is the key-
To have everything-just my own Family.

A Memorable Year

Memories are fleeting little pictures in our minds that
bring back to us the places and the times we left
behind-
Sights and sounds of yesterdays shared moments of me
and you-
The starry nights and bright warm days from when our
love was new-
The catkins by the forest track first heralds of the spring-
The first green shoots on branches bare new life for
everything-
Our forest walks in springtime no words were needed
then-
The peace that we encountered will be with us once
again-
The Bluebells filled the air with scent and as far as we
could see, the
azure coloured carpet bid us sit awhile and be-
At peace with Natures bounty along with badger, fox and
deer-
The air of expectation and renewal every year.

The hazy days of summer brought us picnics by the
stream-

Where damsel flies laid precious eggs watched by the
    silver bream-
The twisted paths along the bank the haunt of water vole-
A heron stands amongst the reeds, a solitary soul-
He works hard for his living in the reed bed standing
    here-
until a passing fish or frog swims past that pointed spear!
Well done 'Jack Hern' you've earned your fill so now
    you're on your
way, we will see you next time we come round your shady
    reedy bay.

Now scents of Autumn fill the air her harvest colours
    bold-
The trees and fields a patchwork of bright reds and
    browns and gold-
The ripened fruits and berries, the waving golden wheat-
a sense of mellow fruitfulness we have enough to eat-
and once more fill the larder with the bounties of the
    yield-
and watch the changing colours in the hedgerow and the
    field-
The trees in autumn dresses of red and brown and gold-
the birds fly south to warmer climes escaping winters
    cold.

The icy fingers of the north and eastern winds will blow-
and shake the rainbow colours from the countryside below-
The naked stems and branches once lush and green and
    fair-
Now glint and sparkle brightly in the frosty morning air-
Like filigree lace the hedgerow wears her necklace if
    glistening
white-
The cattle gather at the barn to shelter for the night-
They settle down in knee deep straw and doze the cold
    away-
Waiting for the warmer winds to keep the chills at bay-

It won't be long before those catkins appear once more in
    the lane-
To let us know that the cycle of spring will soon be around
    again.

The Rolling Stone

The Rolling Stone rolled on and on never staying in one
    place for too long, but
enjoying the lure of all the bright young stones around
    him with their rich glossy
colours, there were fiery red Garnets, lustrous Pearls,
    slinky green Emeralds, cool
blue Topaz, and the sophisticated black Onyx.
He wined and dined them all and moved on to the next
    one without so much as a
backward glance, but, sometimes somehow he felt there
    was always something
missing in his life-

One day as he was rolling along beside a stream that was
    lined with willow trees he
saw them dipping their weeping branches in the cooling
    water as it babbled and
trickled its merry way down to meet the sea. It was there
    by the root of a willow tree
that he spotted half hidden a rather ordinary looking stone
    half covered by moss, but,
when the branches above swayed in the breeze and the
    sun shone brightly on the little

stone she shimmered and glittered in the dappled warmth
    of the sun's rays brighter
than any star. He was captivated by her shy and simple
    grace and he felt compelled
to rest awhile alongside her soft mossy side-

They stayed like that a long time until the Rolling Stone
    felt the need to roll along had
passed, he had finally found a place to rest and spend his
    time with his very own
special little stone and you will still find him there today
    lying under a coat of moss
alongside his little 'Diamond'-

The Lonely Grass

At the end of the road where the Bungalows are, there is a
  place where the grass is
never cut but left to grow wild. An old wooden fence
  separates it from the well cut
manicured lawns of the houses either side of the road.
One of the wild grasses grew tall enough to peer over the
  fence at the smart well cut
grass on the other side but was laughed at and told 'You
  are untidy and straggly and
you live amongst weeds, you are not like us and we don't
  want you here in this smart road!

The little grass was very sad and lonely and wished that
  the man with the mower
would come and cut her down so she could be like the
  well cut manicured lawn next
door, but however she continued to grow and when
  summer came she grew tall
enough to look out over the countryside around her and a
  friendly tree dropped a
branch to shade her from the heat of the midday sun,
  unlike the short cut lawns who
had no shade and became dry and brown and sad.

The wild grass was now tall and graceful with flowering
  seed heads swaying in the
breeze, and, when Autumn came the seeds ripened and a
  flock of tiny birds came and
pecked at the seeds the grass had grown and as they fed
  they twittered and sang to
keep her company and she was very happy that she was
  indeed a wild grass and not
cut down and dry, and she felt sorry for those lawn grasses
  who couldn't see the
countryside around them or be in the shade of a tree or
  have friendly birds to chatter
and peck at their seeds, so she stretched out and leant over
  the fence and dropped
some seeds on the garden the other side,-

I wonder if they will grow?

Master Kung

The wise old Sage Master Kung was sitting in the shade of
the cherry blossom tree
overlooking the valley below and the distant hills beyond
when a Chinese peasant
approached him, and bowing low the man said "Oh
Master Kung I am Sung Lee and
I have travelled a long and difficult journey over rough
and harsh terrain, I come
from the Schuan Province in the south and it has taken
me many many days to reach
you. I have had little to eat or drink and I have left my
wife and family far behind me. My feet are bleeding
and sore having brought me so many miles to see you,
have
you some wise words to say to me oh Master as you sit in
the shade of the Cherry Blossom tree?"

Master Kung raised his hand and bid the peasant come
forward. "Young man you
say that you have travelled many many miles on foot on
harsh and stony ground over
many days, you have left your wife and family far behind

in Schuan Province so you
could visit me here, you are hungry and thirsty and your
    feet are bleeding and sore.
Come sit with me awhile and we will sip tea and eat of the
    fruits of the valley below,
we will discuss many things under the shade of the
    Cherry Blossom tree and you will
rest your weary feet awhile because you see my friend-
I Have No Feet...

Retirement

Welcome to the elite ranks of the ancient and bewildered!
We may not remember what we had for breakfast, but ask
us a question about
1950 or 1960 etc and we are right on it!

Modern technology may not be our thing, but, give us a
ball of string and some bendy twigs and we will whip
up a pair of snow shoes before you can blink, the fact
that we don't need snow shoes is irrelevant!!

Oh the days of nodding off in the middle of your
favourite television programme, or snuggling down in
a nice warm bed and then remembering you forgot to
take your teeth out and put 'em' to soak!

The halcyon days of the free bus pass when you can take
    off at will and never
bother about small change ever again, freedom to visit
    wherever takes your fancy, to be fair you will probably
    forget why you came in the first place, but that's all part
    of the adventure and its free!!

These are just a few of the delights that await you in this
    exclusive club, I would you
tell you about a lot more, but I've forgotten…

To the Tree
in my Garden

You remind me of many happy hours spent in the
    company of the old woody friends
of my childhood, the soft earth under my feet, the smell
    of sun dried leaves as they
fall softly creating the myriad colours of the autumn
    carpet, the sense of mellow
fruitfulness of a good season.

The little fledglings once encompassed in the strong
    woody arms and hands now
flown to warmer climes, but they will return to raise
    another brood next year safe in
the knowledge that the trees will still be here waiting for
    them whispering as the
breeze blows through their leaves creating conversations
    only they understand.

Many a time have I sat amongst the branches twixt
    heaven and earth and dreamed
my dreams or sat beneath in the dappled shade on a hot
    sultry day listening to the
rustle of tiny feet in the undergrowth that the world
    never sees as it passes by.

The bony skeletons appear sullen and silent when the
    Northeasterly winds do blow,
but are transformed into delicate glistening tracery by
    winter's icy hand, like jewels
they patiently await the rebirth of spring, – strong –
    welcoming – and always –
    'there'…

My Mantra for Each Day

It is not the quantity of life that we have on this planet,
but the quality of the time that
we spend together. When in a life threatening situation,
the ability to overcome that
trauma is to try and remember the only thing to fear is
Fear itself!
All knowledge is power so find out all you can about your
'enemy' and don't let the
feeling of helplessness overwhelm you.

You cannot win the war, but, you will find that it comes
via the way of many little
battles and obstacles every day which if taken as individual
obstacles can be
overcome or at least improved enough to make a
difference.
Yesterday is gone, tomorrow is yet to be, Today is here…

Do not be governed by the things that you cannot do,
think of what you can do when
you look closer at your situation and break down some of
the obstacles you may find

you can see things for example…

Q-I cannot walk far any more, no more country rambles
A-I can still drive/be driven to a quiet spot and enjoy the
    scenery/picnic etc…

Q-I cannot work, no holidays or decent income…
A-I can still make a useful contribution by discussions and
    decision making…

Q-I feel unsure of things and places, and I have no
    confidence in anything any more…
A-The mind has the ability to overcome the uncertainty,
    and confidence comes with
Recognition of ones capabilities…

Q-I feel guilty about you being in this situation because of
    me…
A-No one is to blame for circumstances beyond our
    control, negative guilt feelings
Are common but don't help…

Q-I am no longer the man/woman that I was…
A-I am still the same person that I always was but with a
    different perspective on my
life now…

But I Can Still

HEAR-Great music-conversations-whats going on in the world around me-bird song.

SEE-Watch a sunrise or sunset with you-see the flowers-watch a movie- the bright
colours of summer-the TV-your smile…

SMELL-The scent of you-the dinner cooking-freshly mown grass-summer nights-fish & chips…

TOUCH-Your cuddles in the morning-pat the dog-soft blankets-a reassuring hug…

FEEL-The sense that you are nearby-your changing moods-your insecurities-the
support of loving friends and family- and a sense of being alive today…

IN SHORT-The life we have is precious like our memories-enjoy the good days and don't become daunted by the bad ones-keep making memories-keep fighting-keep
living!…

Letting Go

They tell me that I must let you go or you will not rest
    peacefully…

When I can no longer see the moon casting her pale
    beams around me or the stars
shining in your bedroom window on your pillow… Then
    I shall let you go…

When I can no longer feel the warmth of the sun on my
    back when I sit on the grass
and remember the picnics we shared in the meadows..
    Then I shall let you go…

When I can no longer watch the birds come to feed on the
    window sill outside the
bedroom and chatter and sing on a cold winters morning
    as they look for you…
Then I shall let you go…

When I can no longer sit in your armchair and feel your
    warmth enclose me where
we shared our precious moments together, you are still in
    the very threads of the
fabric... Then I shall let you go...

When I can no longer sense that you are here waiting for
    me when I return from
some errand and all is cold and empty... Then I shall let
    you go...

When there is nothing and all is dark and silent and the
    world stops.. Then I will never let you go again because
    I will be with you...

Loss

Are you still here with me my love, around me,
    encompassing me, alongside me
every moment?
Does our love reach across the great abyss to unite us once
    again in some spiritual
form?
I sense your presence everywhere, but I can no longer see
    you, or hold you, or love
you body and soul, and yet the memory of our love brings
    such bitter sweet pain to
my heart.

Don't ever take this pain from me as it is all that I have left
    of you. If I go away, will you still be here when I come
    back? Or will I find the icy coldness of your leaving
without a trace?

I know that I must let you go, but not yet, not yet.
I saw the first catkins today and I cried remembering how
    I used to bring you the
first of every flower I saw when Spring made her
    appearance, be it a Snowdrop,
Primrose, Bluebell, Daffodil or Catkin and bring them to
    put alongside you to cheer
you,

Now I go to put them on your grave…

Granny

Chapter
(1)

Granny was not a handsome woman in fact her nose and chin seemed to meet in the middle rather like the joker on a pack of cards! Her past life and family history was rather sketchy to say the least! Apparently she was of Irish descent and as a young girl was an excellent shot with an air rifle and managed to bag the odd pheasant or rabbit from the nearest estate with ease. One night she met a sea Captain in the pub and he was so impressed with her that he proposed to her on the spot saying "You are the only woman for me because you can drink me under the table and still remain standing! What a girl you'll do for me!

They spent many happy years together and while he was away at sea (which was most of the time) Granny was kept busy looking after the homestead, she would sit in the front porch smoking her old clay pipe and shooting the occasional sparrow off the rooftop to feed her ferrets. Her favourite was a big polecat ferret she named Temoshenko (after the Russian leader) and she was often seen scouring the warrens on the downs above the village. This particular day she was crossing the railway line on her way to the downs when Temoshenko leapt out from the pocket of her jacket and decided to hunt a burrow right under the track itself, unfortunately, the 8.45am train was due at the time so Granny had to think fast to save her favourite polecat. She quickly tore off a strip from her red petticoat and tied it to her walking stick, she then hurried 100yds up the track and stuck the red flag in the middle of the tracks to warn the driver to stop.

In due course the old steam train puffed around the bend and screeched to a halt 6ins from the red flag. The driver jumped out and ran along the track to where Granny was trying to dig out Temoshenko from the burrow underneath the railway line.
He was not best pleased at having to brake hard and spill the passengers tea all over them, eventually however after a long tussle Granny managed to dig Temoshenko out of the burrow with his teeth still attached to the rump of a big buck rabbit and a look of triumph on his face! After apologies all round and the promise of one of Grannies rabbit stews order was again restored and Granny went on her merry way.

Chapter
(2)

It was a bright morning and Granny had been up before dawn as usual, she always said to be in bed when the sun was up was a waste of half a day!
She was going fishing and armed with a bamboo stick, bent pin, thin string and cheese sandwiches (to eat and use as bait) and a flagon of cider she set off with 12 noisy children it tow each carrying their own 'fishing rod' and a good selection of worms freshly dug for the occasion. Their destination the river bordering the old stone quarry where it was said a monster brown trout called 'The General' lurked in the shadowy reedy depths, no one had ever caught him or in fact even seen him but it was enough to stir the imagination of the prospective invasion of local fisher folk of all ages! Soon the chattering stopped as each small head was intent on fixing worm to pin and casting into the flowing depths of the river.

The sun was hot and Granny was dozing after a sip of cider and a sandwich when all hell broke loose as a fight occurred on the river bank as two boys hooked into what appeared to be 'The General' and each tugged hard at their lines, unfortunately, both lines broke and much anger was unleashed with the spectators cheering on their own 'champion', of course all the commotion drove any prospective catch a mile up the river. Granny however had the solution, she produced from her pocket a large slab of toffee she had made especially for the fishing trip and taking command of the situation made sure every fisherman had a large portion of toffee which unknown to the hungry horde was especially difficult to chew but very tasty so the effort required to finally conquer and swallow the said toffee was to say the least extreme – soon silence prevailed once more and when respective parents came to collect their offspring at tea time they found them asleep dotted all along the riverbank, and Granny quietly puffing away at her pipe with enough fish for all in the creel by her side.

Chapter
(3)

It was harvest time and Granny was busy foraging in the fields and hedgerows for her winter store of elderberries, crab apples, blackberries, rose petals and hips. All these goodies were taken back to the homestead and transformed into all the delicacies that reminded everyone of their country childhood. Of course there were no 'fridges' in her day so preserves were the order of the day Elder flowers made good fritters nice and crisp, also elderflower champagne (a sparkling refreshing cordial on a hot day) whilst the berries made good jam either on their own or mixed with apples resembling blackcurrants in taste and texture. Blackberries of course made jam-pies and tarts. Rose petals for jam delicate in taste rather like Turkish delight in flavour. All these bounties of Nature were transformed in Grannies kitchen!

This particular day however she was in the fields gleaning for any seed that was left behind after harvesting the wheat and barley which Granny collected to feed her chickens. As she walked through the pasture alongside the barley field she noticed a naked male rump in the grass, making her way towards the undulating spectacle she gave it a sharp prod with her walking stick saying "don't forget to shut the gate on your way out young man" and carried on without even breaking her stride! Nothing in Nature ever phased her but no doubt the magic of the moment was completely lost on the unfortunate couple!

The weather was extremely hot and a sudden summer thunderstorm erupted,
everyone made for the cover of the nearby woods except Granny who just put her
shawl over her head and carried on. Suddenly there was a flash of lightning and
Granny fell to the ground having been struck down by the bolt. Everyone rushed over fearing the worst but Granny was not daunted by a stroke of lightning, she got to her feet and smoothed down her skirts and when asked if she was alright she replied,
"Well, it just goes to show that at 80 years old I'm still attractive"…

Chapter
(4)

Granny was unique to say the least, before the days of 'Sat Nav' she found her way at night by starlight and position of the sun by day. If it was cloudy she would sniff the wind like an old dog fox and her inbuilt sense of direction never failed her, she would say: – "If you don't know where you are and you don't care where you are you can never be lost!"

Her knowledge of plants and their uses (handed down through the generations) was phenomenal, no modern pills or potions for Granny, Mother Nature will provide was her dictum. She could swing a 9lb wood axe as well as any man, or sew a button or repair a dress with stitches as neat as any sewing machine.

Her shiny little homestead welcomed all comers whatever their religion, origin, class or position in life. Her own life was governed by the seasons of the year and her philosophy was to simplify life and retain the same 'joie de vie' and curiosity all her days. She asked not for much just a space to grow and wildlife for company and she was content with her horde of little followers and those older ones who came to her for sound advice on any problem under the sun.

She was no pushover and would fight her corner with gusto when the need arose.

She remained active all her life and when she reached
the great age of 100 years, the
local press came to interview her and asked her to what
did she owe her long life and what advice did she have
for the young generation to enable them to live long
and happy lives?
Granny surveyed the eager crowd hanging on her every
word and with a twinkle in her eye she said, "If you
wish to live a long and happy life I suggest that you just
keep breathing."

Well done Granny, rest in peace surrounded by the
nature that you loved so much.

Now where did I put that old clay pipe?

FOR
KING
AND
COUNTRY

For King and Country

THE BEGINNING

This is the story of a young man, very ordinary, who became a very Ordinary Seaman. In 1939, the Dogs of War were unleashed from their kennels. By Press, Placard, and Proclamation, the citizens of England were urged to 'do their bit' Prepare for War and Dig for Victory. The evocative words of World War One poet Rupert Brooke echoed around us, 'Now God be thanked who has matched us with his hour, and caught our youth and wakened us from our slumbers...' I awoke and promptly joined the Royal Navy.

Qualifying as a Gunlayer in that Mecca of gunnery Whale Island Portsmouth I yearned to strike a blow for my King and Country and the Royal Navy of course!
Well nourished on a diet of Drake, Hawkins, Anson and Nelson, my modest desire was to create havoc on enemy warships. In so doing I hoped to be Decorated, Promoted Saluted and finally enter the history books as the 'Saviour of England and her stout people'.

To my consternation neither King, Country, Royal Navy nor anything else appeared to appreciate my zeal and patriotism!

Requesting on the correct form a draft to any Battleship in need of a keen Gunner, I awaited the rush of great Men-0-War requiring my services! My Lords of Admiralty (or their minions) had other ideas. They pitch forked me upon the deck of a 'Minesweeper.' This ancient rust bucket a converted trawler lay quietly in an east coast harbour. Her crew of ex-fishermen tough, taciturn and tactless, swarmed over her like blowflies on a corpse! We prepared provisioned and painted, then, we went to War. Our duty was plain, to act in groups to sweep vital shipping lanes and channels for enemy mines. If attacked by enemy aircraft to shoot back, if we were bombed or mined 'Hard luck' it was as simple as that!

In those halcyon days, Regular Naval cooks had not made their appearance on these 'little ships' thus we seadogs had to cook by rotation, the effect could be stimulating to say the least! When my name appeared on top of the list in the galley I was excited by the thought of promotion. However my hopes were soon dashed by the Petty Officer, "Promotion lad, duty cook matey that's what you are, and remember we want good plain food we are Lowestoft fishermen and we like big suet dumplings or over the side you'll go." I promised to do my best.

The dumpling when mixed was the size of a large bolster, a clean dustbin its cradle. The P.O. went on "wrap it up in cloth, cover it with water and let it simmer until it lifts the lid off, stick your fork in it and if the fork comes out easy then she's ready. So get cracking! And another thing, we like lots of gravy with our roast beef and don't forget good strong tea to wash it down."

The monstrous pudding was duly wrapped by me in clean 'sailcloth' and consigned to the depths of the dustbin. Our ship rolled, wallowed, and heaved in and over grey North Sea waves. The galley was very hot. Steam issued from leaking valves, bubbles of sweat dripped from my forehead, nose and chin to bounce and spit on the hotplate.

After some time, I raised the dustbin lid to see how my creation was progressing. Like a
Jack-in-the-box the huge pudding shot to the surface. Alas! The canvas sailcloth had prevented the water from penetrating the pudding, (a pudding I was now beginning to hate with every fibre of my being). Rushing to the foc'sle I rummaged in a locker and selected a soft fairly clean flotilla football jersey, this was more like it I thought!

Soon my creation was happily gurgling away in its new coat until the moment of truth dawned…

❧

At the appointed time, off came the lid in went the fork and out came the pudding. To my utter surprise the cloth was now a lead colour, and the suet pudding/dumpling a bright strawberry red! It was plain to see that the dye had run into the mixture, one football jersey now grey blue was hurriedly dispatched to 'Davy Jones locker'!

The leading seaman of the mess came forth with a cheery greeting, "Something smells good cooky, I'm bloody starving lets have the grub out."

On seeing the scarlet object steaming quietly on its tray, he stopped short, "Christ mate, what's that? We've never had a pudd like that before." Sweating more than ever I gulped, "Ah this is a special colouring its called cochineal my old granny used to use it a lot, take it below while its hot, tell 'em roast beef is on its way."

He tottered away staring hard at the pudding now glowing like a tropical sunset.

The great joint of beef (due to luck more than judgement) was done to a turn, remembering the PO's words, I looked everywhere in the galley for gravy browning without success. The tins on the shelves had no labels, however, one large canister I found was full of what appeared to be 'Bisto' powder. With gusto I mixed it and spooned it over the joint in great measure. They want lots of gravy then by God they'll have it!

The crisp succulent joint with its escort of plump roast potatoes, was soon dispatched to its destination, the seamen's mess. A gallon of piping hot tea as thick as treacle followed the culinary cortege.

Eight bells rung (mid-day) and my ordeal for a while was over. I was too exhausted to eat myself after being locked in mortal combat with the pudding, so, sipping weak tea well sweetened with ships condensed milk, I thought those human gannets would by now be busy scoffing the meal so carefully prepared. I wished them good luck good health and good fortune!

At 1400 hours, surprisingly, coloured bunting fluttered out from the signal halyards. Our ship suddenly left her station with the flotilla to turn around!

We returned to harbour. On the jetty a gaggle of sick berth ratings and an ambulance awaited us. To my amazement I saw my shipmates stagger from the foc'sle. These tough weather beaten seadogs looked pale, weary, and unusually silent. They were bound for the naval sick quarters. Two other shore personnel came aboard and examined my utensils in the galley taking away the tin of 'bisto' gravy browning and me!

Quite simply as events unfolded, the story was this: Sometime after gorging themselves on my victuals, pain and stomach disorder hit them one by one. Our skipper had no alternative but to request his superior's permission to return to harbour. 'Suspected poisoning' was his reason for so drastic a step! Later it was shown that the culprit was the gravy browning. In effect the powder was brick dust and colzaline oil used (with brasso) to polish the ships brass, a very important part of naval routine! Naturally I was the prime suspect…

Ashore I faced the base captain, who at once fired verbal broadside after broadside at me, his reasoning was plain to see.

He suggested that having been denied the opportunity for 'big ship' gunnery duty and finding myself on board a disreputable trawler I intended seeking revenge, after all, was it not significant (on my own admission) he went on, "You did not partake of the mid-day meal Yourself? For the first time in the annals of Naval Warfare he said a British ship of War had to return to harbour without firing a shot in anger. You have in fact done more damage to the War effort than the enemy! What say you?"

"Not guilty sir," I replied, "It was I submit an error of judgement in good faith. Due to lack of labels or definitions of contents on the galley tins, that is all sir."

His verdict was given in due course. No evidence of intent could be proven against me; however, I was to be removed from the vessel as a precautionary measure. To be drafted back to Portsmouth, to be given disciplinary drill and kept 'hard at it.' Under no circumstances was I to be allowed anywhere near kitchens or galleys! To await the Drafting Commanders pleasure, whence he hoped a suitable ship could be found in a more active theatre of war. I thanked him but was abruptly ordered to keep silent, muster my effects and prepare an immediate journey to Portsmouth. "This was necessary," he went on to protect me from reprisals. "You must realise you have made quite a few enemies amongst the trawler fraternity, they are a close community and I should hate to learn that someone has fished your body out of the dock! Now leave this base at once your train is already in the station!

For King and Country

⚘

THEATRE OF WAR

My journey to Portsmouth was fairly uneventful, just a few Air raids! A pleasant change from the voice of my former Base Captain, which had resounded like the bark of a 16' gun all sound and fury.

After a period in limbo, the 'powers that be' in their infinite wisdom found me a corvette in Liverpool. Unfortunately she was only based there, spending most of her time ploughing the Atlantic Ocean on convoy duty.

The Battle of the Atlantic was at its height, my Gunnery Officer encouraged, nay, implored me to shoot at the enemy as often as I could. "You see," he wisely explained, "you will never get a better chance to fire off as many shells, of course they are expensive but we don't pay for 'em! When this war ends (if indeed you live to see that day) shotgun cartridges will cost you dear. Make the most of your chance now, indeed, the Admiralty insists that you blaze away for your King and Country!" I promised to do my best for all concerned.

I will not bore the reader with my personal account of the Battle of the Atlantic, (modesty forbids it), but I agree wholeheartedly with Sir Winston Churchill who said it was, "A battle of Science and Seamanship, of Ambush and Ambuscade, of death by groping and drowning, groping I didn't mind, But drowning!

One morning I awoke with a revelation, it was as if I had 'seen the light.' It occurred to me that if I was to give my life for King and Country then it ought to be in much warmer water than the implacable, cold, menacing Atlantic Ocean. Not an unreasonable request surely? I felt that the Admiralty would definitely see my point of view; they usually did if the request was sincere, truthful, and above all written on the correct form!

With undue haste my request was presented to my commanding officer. Short and sweet it merely requested that I be drafted as soon as possible to the 'Mediterranean Theatre of War.' My reason for this was plain; it would be of great help to me in my post war career as a student of Classical History!

In due course, (and to my utter amazement), it was granted. I praised the Almighty and the Royal Navy for having such faith in my services and devotion to duty. After all, I had been given not only their approval but also their blessing!

My Captain wished me good luck, (adding I must confess) "the ship's company will not be sorry to see you leave." However, the euphoric cloud which had enveloped me soon dissolved when I discovered I was to be drafted (not to the Mediterranean) but to Scapa Flow for convoy duties in Russian waters!

Disappointment descended upon me, this must surely be a 'clerical error' (not unknown in service life!) Voicing my dismay to my ships regulating Petty Officer, he replied in his usual understanding gentle tone, "Perhaps for you lad it's a step in the right direction!"

The Fleet M.O. lectured us new arrivals on the unpleasant effects of frostbite and V.D! He cheerfully told us that should we fall overboard, "death will be swift, you will be frozen solid in five minutes, stiff as a railway sleeper. Any questions?"

"Yes Sir," I piped up, "What time is the next train to London?" Result, five days punishment for a frivolous remark during a war time lecture, not a good start!…

The trips to Murmansk and Archangel were rather trying to say the least! Fog enveloped us, great green glassy mountains of seawater swept over us. Frost that turned the slender halyards to rigid white telegraph poles. The cold, so intense that it bored like a rat into your very vitals, this was cheerfully known as the 'chill factor.'

Long range German Condor aircraft shadowed us relentlessly in conjunction with U Boats. Ship after ship would explode in a pall of flame and dense black smoke. Intense cold and fatigue played strange tricks on me. At times our company of merchant ships and escorts would float silently away into white walls of fog. We would feel abandoned, alone, and apprehensive. Ships seemed to be suspended in great cotton wool globes, expanding then contracting without shape or form. Often I believed we and our consorts would be destined to sail these ghostly waters for all eternity, lost for ever, great phantom ships of war circling sea, sky, the very universe. This thought I did not relish! Something would have to be done, but what? How? Escape from these waters was impossible, unless (as Admiralty put it) they discharged you 'dead' and dutifully stamped your kit bag D.D.

Every attempt to malinger was catalogued with naval expertise, and culprits severely dealt with. There 'must' be a way for me to get through to the Admiralty, but it wasn't going to be easy. It had to be something that even those 'sea eagles' hadn't heard of, hadn't a ready reply to or seen it in their vast manuals compiled since King Alfred's day… Thus I reasoned and once again I submitted a request form to my Commander!

Now the Admiralty liked to see request forms completed correctly. They must never be frivolous, always readable, short and above all simple. I obeyed these orders scrupulously. Request: Permanent duty in Russian waters! (just that) no more and certainly no less. The Commander frowned and flinched, the Master-at-Arms peeping over his shoulder turned a shade paler. At last the Commander with a voice like brittle glass said, "Request held over, carry on."

Later on our return to Scapa Flow, the Master-at-Arms crisply barked, "You mate are going ashore, a signal has arrived, you will report to the base Medical Officer, here comes the 'trot boat' alongside, Jump to it!"

"But I don't want to go ashore," I replied, "I'm quite happy aboard, I can't wait to push off for Murmansk again, you saw my request for permanent duty in Russian waters, I want to stay with my shipmates."

"Not if I can help it lad," he spat out, "you're as nutty as a fruit cake! Get dressed in number ones 'Now' that's an order."

I was ushered into a large very warm room in Base Sick Quarters. Three medical officers sat at the well-polished table. I felt rather ill at ease, and thought to break the tension I would compliment the most senior and imposing doctor on the warmth and general tidiness of his office. Peering long and hard at me over his spectacles, he said quietly, "Do you know who I am?"

Replying in all sincerity I said, "Do you mean to say that you don't know who you are sir? I know who I am." He tapped the four gold rings on his sleeve, saying, "Look at these," I stood petrified for some time. He then said, "Are you dumb man? For God's sake say something."

Spluttering nervously I answered, "they look very nice sir" (and tapping my own overlong sleeves) "and look what they have given me sir!"

I was told to wait in an adjoining room. A sick berth P.O. brought me in a meal. Asking him who the senior fellow was who had tapped his four gold rings for me to look at, he replied,
"He is the consulting psychiatrist, a clever bloke too, be careful what you say to him he's a tricky customer!"

Resuming my interview, the psychiatrist said, "I understand you wish to remain in Russian waters, why?"

"Because I like it sir."

"What do you like about it?"

"It's the sense of space sir and the coloured lights, the Aurora Borealis and it's all free too."

"What about the 'other lights' star shells, bombs, torpedoes etc?"

"Ah that's artificial not the same sir!"

He continued, "Do you realise the life expectancy of an escort vessel such as yours is only twelve weeks?"

"I hadn't given it much thought sir."

"Are you really telling me that you want to die?"

"Of course sir!"

"You are abnormal, no one in his right mind wants to die, don't you agree?"

"Not quite sir, I replied, "you see every time I travel through our cities and towns, I see large posters all over the walls saying… 'Give your life for King and Country, join the Royal Navy etc,' so that's why I joined the Royal Navy Sir for the privilege to do what was asked of me."

"That is a morbid, unhealthy attitude," he replied.

"Does that mean I cannot give my life for the cause then sir?"

"Certainly not, 'we' will decide what is best for you, you will not lay down your life, or anything else, unless we say so! Is that quite clear? Although we sympathise with your beliefs and strong desire to offer yourself as a sacrificial lamb, on no account are you to be allowed to carry out your wish. That's an order! Tell me," he went on, "what else would you like to do, apart from this 'cock and bull' story of permanent duty in Russian waters?"

"I would like to drop by parachute in the heart of Berlin, Sir."

"Why Berlin?"

"To assassinate Hitler, after all he started it, I would like to finish it!"

"Have you ever been dropped by parachute before?" he asked.

"No Sir, but I could learn, I may only be five feet eight inches tall, but I am sturdy!"

As a matter of interest, how precisely do you intend to assassinate Herr Hitler?"

"I haven't quite made up my mind yet sir, I need more time to plan the details."

Thumbing through my service records, the consultant murmured, "You seem to be well acquainted with poison! I understand you almost succeeded in wiping out a whole ships company at Lowestoft, something about substances placed in the food when you were duty cook in a minesweeper. I feel sure my Lords of Admiralty could never accept the services of a modern day 'Crippen' in the Royal Navy, furthermore, it is contrary to the Geneva Convention. Sorry to disappoint you young man but I am of the opinion you need a long rest! You will be sent to a convalescent home in the country until further notice. No more Russian convoys, or foolish ideas such as giving your life for King and Country, until we give permission of course! That is an order!"

Even now as I retreat down the long highway of memory to the dark days of War, one thing still puzzles me; Everyone urged me to 'give my life for King and Country,' yet, everyone in authority did their best to prevent me from doing 'just that'.

For King and Country

ﾟ

IDEAS TO SHORTEN THE WAR

After my enforced 'holiday' along the South Coast, I eventually received a 'missive' report once again for sea duty.

A long and weary journey to northern Scotland brought me to my new ship-of-war. Anti-submarine vessel, a former deep-sea trawler. I was to be her Gun layer. My new Captain (LT).r.n.v.r. was keen, young and itching to grapple with the foe! In civil life he was a stockbroker! Perusing my travel documents, he barked, "Guns, your service record is disgusting. You are a disgrace to your uniform!"

"Thank you sir," I replied.

"Keep silence," he shouted. "Pay attention to what I say."

"Of course, sir."

Warming to his subject, he remarked, "You, are one of natures casualties, thus expendable, however depend upon it, 'I will soon lick you into shape, you will strike a blow for England and thus redeem yourself,' Understand?"

"Quite so sir."

He then proceeded to read quotations from Drake,

Grenville, Anson and Nelson, then ordered me to 'get a haircut.' (He would definitely need watching.) He departed muttering something about the sweepings of every Naval establishment!

Dress on Naval trawlers was generally less rigid than on say Battleships. As befits an old Wykhamist, my Captain was immaculate at all times; he even shaved twice a day! Our Coxswain wore a velvet smoking jacket with carpet slippers when at the wheel! The Signal man (r.n.v.r.) and a former B.B.C. cameraman sported a bow tie! However, our Telegraphist was a real character! Classical Scholar, (double first at Oxford,) fluent in Greek, Latin, and Persian to boot! Also, he was a well-known 'drummer' in society circles with a yen for Latin American 'jungle beats.' In his Harrods blue silk dressing gown he tapped away at his Morse keys. Often, he would lapse into his 'jungle rhythms' (much to the alarm of Fleet Signal Officers!) One thing at least, I told him, no enemy intelligence monitor could ever break your individual messages! Alas, (neither could we.)

My weapons too were unusual. One four inch gun (1916 vintage,) four Lewis guns, one Orklikon, two Hotchkiss (on the Bridge,) six 303 rifles (as used up the Khyber Pass,) four Webley .45 revolvers, some depth charges, primers, Very pistols and a brace of Holman's bomb projectors thrown in for good measure!

Thus we went to War. In the far-flung wastes of those cold, turbulent seas and winds of the Northern Patrol, we bucketed and retched in search of the foe.

Early one morning, (in a snowstorm and force eight wind) our Captain cleared lower deck:

"Now chaps," he piped, ""I have some exciting news, news that we have all been waiting for. The Admiralty informs me that the German Battleship 'Bismarck' has left Norway and is probably in our area. We must keep a sharp lookout for her, so, to your battle stations, 'guns,' report to me in my cabin." He soon came to the point! "My plan of action," he went on "is bold, imaginative and best of all, simple! The weather is our ally; we will creep up under Bismarck's stern 'guns".

"Is that wise sir? I queried, "All she needs to do is throw a few grenades down on us!"

"Do not question your Captain that's an order! Bismarck's freeboard is so high she could never train even her secondary guns on us, is that clear?"

"Of course, Sir," I replied.

"Now your job 'guns' is to blow her rudder off when we creep under her stern, thus 'crippled' she will soon be demolished by our heavy Battleships now in hot pursuit. Do you think you can register a hit?"

"No problem Sir, after all she is a fairly large target! I feel rather like a randy Fox Terrier trying to mount an elephant!"

"Enough obscenity 'guns,' remember if you can bring this off, a medal will certainly be yours. Not to mention you will personally shake the hand of the Commander-in-Chief. Another thing, do not under any circumstances shoot until you see my battle pennant hoisted. My Lords of Admiralty insist on the strict observance of the 'Rules of

Engagement' we cannot open fire until our Battle Pennant is hoisted correctly! Now, any questions 'guns?'"

"Suppose Sir, just suppose they sink us first before I open fire whilst waiting for your Battle Pennant to be raised?"

"In that case 'guns,' my Lords of Admiralty will never ever forgive or forget you. Should we go down, and should you be picked up from the 'drink' by one of our rescue ships, then plead insanity (that should be no problem for you!) Do I make myself clear?"

"Of course Sir, perfectly clear," I replied.

"To your gun platform at the double, and remain there. You will be sent a bucket of tea, bread, and one extra sausage!"

"Thanks awfully Sir, most kind."

"Enough impertinence 'guns,' remember your promotion prospects depend on me! Now away to your place of duty."

Later, much later, a great dark shape (big as Battersea power station) loomed over us as she emerged from the fog! Our Coxswain immediately put the wheel hard over. Three times we charged at her stern, and three times she avoided us. The bridge to gun platform phone shrilled, "Shoot guns Shoot you idiot, can't you see my battle pennant, the Captain screamed:

"Unable to train on her Sir, she's too evasive," I replied. "Can we ram her instead?"

Suddenly a voice boomed out across the waves, "This is the Battleship King George V speaking, we are not playing rounders Captain, why are you chasing me? Do you require a tow? If not return to base at once, we are in pursuit of Bismarck, and Captain, please inform your gun layer in his filthy jersey this is not, repeat not, an inter-service football match! Over and out…"

For King and Country

∼

The war at sea intensified. Ships large and small plunged into the abyss of a watery grave. They took with them food, oil, minerals and metals. They took the men who sailed in them, men who were the very substance of our islands lifeblood.

The Battle of the Atlantic raged by day and night. As one who took part in this battle, I can testify to the horror, the weariness, and the futility of getting to grips with a ruthless and implacable pack of steel wolves, (the U-boat packs) which straddled the sea routes. Helped by long-range aircraft (and the lack of escort vessels for our convoys) they attacked at will.

Nature was often against the so-called 'righteous.'

Waves green and grey, tall as stockpiled coal heaps battered the thin sides of our ships. The loud metallic drumbeats of Depth Charges assailed our ears as we tried to snatch an hour's sleep.

Dawn broke; we rubbed our bloodshot eyes encrusted with salt. Our food ran short as we doubled to and fro on extended searches. The sea erupted with one, two, even three explosions as great oil tankers burned like monstrous volcanic infernos, blistering our paintwork as we tried to approach them.

Once again the U-boats sprang their tactical trap. Once again Britain lost more of her lifeblood, namely her valiant seamen.

Alas, everything comes to an end. We said goodbye to our rust-streaked old 'Merchantmen.' Those defiant, gallant ships and crews, now decreasing day by day. We slid gently into our berth, limping with our weariness and the burden of our responsibility.

We 'cleaned ship,' ourselves, and I secured all guns.

Later, the Captain sent for me. "Guns," he said, "I believe you would like to see this war end?"

"I would not object to that Sir," I remarked.

"You surprise me 'guns'," he replied, after all, you appear to be thoroughly enjoying expending hundreds of rounds of bullets and shells at several quid a throw! Mind you, to be fair we are never short of 'ammo,' someone has to get 'em' up in the air, might as well be you, what do you say to that?"

"I agree Sir, my training has paid off. My gunnery school 'motto' was: Get 'em' away fast, never let 'em' go stale or get tarnished. Make a loud noise, (it impresses the witnesses!) Remember, Gunnery ratings are a bulldog breed, gait and gaiters, renowned from Portsmouth to Patras. We are chosen to draw the gun carriage on the death of Kings! We go to heaven eventually, unlike seamen, stewards, and telegraphists!

"Precisely 'guns'," the Captain interposed, "It is just possible that unless you get your shooting act together, we shall all end up in that ethereal paradise sooner than we expect! It is one thing to snipe at wretched seagulls dozing on fairway buoys, or 'fire at will' on miserable old R.A.F. Handley Page Hampden planes, quite another to destroy a pack of U-boats!"

"The trouble is Sir," I replied, "They never give me a sporting chance, they never show themselves on the surface for long enough."

"Quite so 'guns,' however, I refer you to a new A.F.O. that has come to my attention! (In fairness to my readers, I will explain.) A.F.Os are Admiralty fleet orders, to be read forthwith by officers and ratings alike. They are ignored at your peril!

Now I never knew who wrote or issued these literary 'gems,' some say Sea Lords and their cohorts write them! However to their credit, even in the darkest hours of the war, A.F.Os were hurled like javelins at every ship and shore establishment from Hong Kong to Hazlemere! This says a lot for the tenacity of my Lords of Admiralty, and their printers! They make pleasant enough reading after a few weeks at sea in the Western Ocean. Often one could find interesting paragraphs, or amendments with lots of oblique strokes and numerical juxtapositions! At times, I preferred them to our Railway timetables; at least they meant what they said.

Nevertheless, my Capt. drew my attention to the very

latest A.F.O. as a most urgent directive from the Prime Minister himself. In effect it was an invitation to anyone anxious to bring the war to a swift conclusion.

It was as if a syndicate of Sea Lords and Scientists said; "You chaps are graciously entreated to submit ideas (however far-fetched) to end the war and knock the enemy for six. Every submission (however idiotic) will be scrutinised by a panel of experts distinguished in formulating active policies from such ideas. Foolscap was to be provided by the writer's branch. No submission will, should, or can be obstructed on its journey to a secret address. Cash awards will be considered, (after hostilities cease!) Each idea will be judged on its own merit, and a chance to see His Majesty pinning a medal on your chest is a strong possibility! "Good luck chaps, and remember Britannia rules the waves." This indeed was heady stuff!

Never have I seen an A.F.O. read with such enthusiasm and euphoria. Normally, the 'lower deck' only read these missives if it was rumoured there may be a rise in pay, or easy (and quick) promotion, but this was different. A master of oratory like Cicero, Demosthenes or even Shakespeare no less, was asking the meek and humble (us!) To 'finish the job' and defeat the accursed 'Hun' (or any other enemy within or without)

Anything, repeat, anything capable of reducing a U-boat or 'Tiger tank, Battleship or Bunker to dust was encouraged. Off with kid gloves, Rules of engagement, Battle pennants and the like were to be put in cold storage! No means fair or foul were to rejected in this plea to up chaps and at 'em.' Our rewards were assured, (if of course we lived long enough to receive them!)

Once more the old British lion stirred and showed its fangs! I at once asked for a bundle of foolscap, (and time off) to compose my 'master stroke.' Foolscap was given willingly, time off 'never.' "That's an order 'guns'," I was told. I mused on the infinite wisdom of the exalted persons who control our Ships of war, and those who man them. For instance, whatever dire, dark, and dangerous threat to our very existence, the Royal Navy never ever runs short of these following items: Paper, Brasso, Bluebell (metal polish) and soap. Only when these items are no more can we truly say that Britannia is no more!

Lacking as I was in a public school education I was forced to rely on common sense in my theory. My effort was to defeat the U-boat by means hitherto untried. To get to grips with these monsters, therefore allowing our Royal Naval gunners to draw first blood. My aim was simplicity, and economic viability, (though neither methods were generally adopted by Government departments!)

Thus in accordance with A.F.O. no: 12/6/41 opened the batting as follows:

"My Lords of Admiralty, your Scientists, and others involved. It seems to me the problem lies in the avoidance of the U-boat Capts to be caught on the surface of British waters. They will not stand and fight! This is typical of the enemy, and is to say the least unsporting and unbritish. However, my plan is novel, simple, cheap and could be devastating in its purging effects on U-boats and their crews, also, it would help to please our housewives knowing they were aiding the war effort!

Our British housewives have in their bathrooms row upon row of 'liver salts' Chemist shops are bursting at the seams with the stuff! I suggest, by act of Parliament, (Defence of the Realm Act) we commandeer every bottle, carton and box. This to be used in special tankers, or propelled rockets, shells and bombs, in the war at sea.

When U-boats are detected amidst a convoy of our ships, and (as usual) skulking beneath the waves, on a secret signal, a vast simultaneous discharge of tons of liver salts is shot into the sea! Result, effervescent bubbling and rise in sea levels would create an artificial surface wave zone. U-boat Capts, (to maintain periscope vision) would 'up scope' and boat. Immediately, the seas bubbling would die down, (after salts activity) and the U-boats would be stranded like sitting ducks on the surface! We, the Royal Navy Gunners, would then eliminate them forever in one foul swoop. It isn't cricket of course, but then neither is torpedoing our ships…

Twelve weeks after my plan was submitted, a reply was sent to me post haste. I was commended on my 'patriotic fervour,' and promised a new ship!

My Lords of Admiralty stated that my plan was impractical (at present;) due to shortage of available bulk liver salts carriers, and the possibility of adverse reaction by the women of Britain! However, my plan was to be filed away in a pigeon hole and I should carry on submitting other interesting ideas to shorten the war!

For King and Country

彡

LOWESTOFT

Travel by train in Wartime was a worthwhile experience, at least I thought so! Others may disagree. Steam, rain, snow, windswept platforms were a welcome relief from ploughing the Atlantic Ocean in a blizzard designed by the Devil himself.

The beauty of Naval life (in an establishment) was the opportunity to get away from it! Notice boards offered a variety of places to visit. Courses in A.A. Gunnery or Submarine detection etc, various lectures on this and that. One could spend an enjoyable two hours looking earnestly at notices. Spring and summer were the best, this green and pleasant land, rich in history, bountiful in beauty, beckoned me to share her treasures, and best of all, a benevolent Government paid in the shape of a travel warrant and a meal bag. The latter was usually one cheese roll, a lettuce leaf, and two glucose sweets.

But no matter, it was a train journey, free, with pleasant porters murmuring, "Close the doors please." Thus I traversed the length and breadth of my native land. Passing great barrage balloons, multi colored washing at the rear of multi colored houses. Over great viaducts, bridges, under tunnels, through cuttings and other railway memorabilia. In due course I became a railway 'buff' and tour adviser to my shipmates. Thanks to the Royal Navy I travelled as much by train as I did by ship!

It is quite possible that I became the best and most knowledgeable rating on every conceivable system of Naval Warfare, solely due to my enthusiasm for travelling to these courses on such interesting topics. My only fear was that one day I would be asked to make use of my new knowledge, or, (and this was more likely,) the Admiralty would run out of courses for me to volunteer for!

The latter happened! A drafting Master-at-Arms sent for me. He said, "Lad, this will hurt you more than me, allow me to give you a 'travel warrant' (no need to tell you how to use it as I understand you are well acquainted with all forms of service transport!) Your presence is required at the Minesweeping Depot Lowestoft. Doubtless you have passed it on your numerous 'free' travels! No need to give 'you' a timetable, you probably even know the type of coal those Eastern engines use! So 'jump to it,' get your meal bag from the NAFFI I don't want to see you again until this bloody war is over!"

Thus, I rattled through the length and breadth of Southern and Eastern England. The tired old engine groaned, spluttered, and complained in its desire to do its duty for our fighting men and women. Mile after mile she ran, crept, or bellowed heavy with her age and the burden of her passengers. Passengers, who in a variety of uniforms slept, dreamt, cried in their sleep, or stood sad faced with rifles and respirators at the ready.

Darkness fell, (and so did a few bombs nearby!) We sheltered under a tunnel, and I tried to memorise 'Dantes Inferno' but could only remember 'Miltons Paradise lost!' Dawn filtered through grimy windows as we chugged into Peterborough West Station. Then we reversed, and chugged back into our tunnel! Apparently, more bombs were falling! This macabre game of railway 'musical chairs' continued via Norwich, until we crept like a long black slug into Lowestoft. The night sky was ablaze with searchlights and pretty red stars cracking away with gusto. It was a barrage of Ack-Ack shells. Once more we reversed and slept the night through down a siding, amidst nestling reeds and waterbeds.

Another dawn fitfully covered the wide expanse of green marshland. I was watching enthralled the glorious plumage of a Kingfisher darting like a jewelled lamp past my carriage window, when our engine snorted, wheezed, and lurched forward. Clang-clang, Clang-clang she panted, over fishplates and steel joints. It was Lowestoft or bust! Come bombers, or the perils of Hell itself, our Driver and Fireman wanted their breakfast! They had had enough, so had their passengers! So too, it seemed had our little engine, for she shuddered and gently expired! Poor thing run into the ground, (over exertion no doubt) She cried out for respite, and a long convalescence in some quiet little siding!

Eventually we all received absolution in the shape of a fussy old tank engine, who prodded and pushed us into Lowestoft. The end of the line, and the end of my long railway saga.

A Bedford truck (RN) awaited us like V.I.Ps en-route to Paradise. We crowded into the well-sprung interior and rumbled into the base. Later, we showered, shaved, and tumbled into the canteen for a meal. Rock buns, Spam sandwiches and tea. Tea, pale, weak, old and cold. I wondered if only I could find a notice board soliciting Naval Personnel to volunteer for say, a six-week course in the Lake District, 'anything would do' for example; Repulsion of German agents by Naval launches! Accommodation provided of course (with trout fishing perhaps!) in a commandeered Guesthouse on the banks of Lake Windermere? Alas, no such luck! I felt sure my Lords of Admiralty would never regret such a project. It would show that the 'Senior Service' had thought of each and every threat to our Sovereign and State! I for one would never jeopardise their trust in me, (and the culling of Deer, Grouse, and fat Trout would help to subsidise the Nations food stocks, or rather those naval members who (by their initiative captured such prey!)

At 1500hrs, I was 'paged.' Would I please report to the 'Billeting Office' at the double. A kindly looking Chief Petty Officer smiled, "Welcome to H.M.S. Europa, any questions?"

"Yes chief, what Barrack block do I sleep in tonight?"

"You don't lad, 'this' is not your pampered 'Pompey.' Here we runs things differently, we ain't got a bleedin' barracks block mate, we billets you me old shipmate. We gives you a 'chit,' you hops in a Bedford truck, and the 'Killick' drops you off at some address. You humps your kit bag and other garbage, and presents your body to the 'Landlady.' It's like a lucky dip, some you win, and some you lose. Then, at 0800hrs, you reports back here for the Parade and Duty Roster. Don't forget it!"

"But suppose Chief," I remarked, "just suppose I don't like the Landlady and her billet? And, it may be a long way out of Lowestoft?"

"Well smart arse," he replied, "In the first place you bloody well lumps it and even marries the Landlady if necessary, and in the second place, you shakes a leg early enough to report 'ere,' or we puts you in 'chokey.' Now, get under way 'chop chop'."

I thanked him for his advice and courtesy!…

Sometime later, I was loaded onto a truck in which three dozen other 'Pilgrims' stood silent, sorrowful, and resentful. "It's like a 'bleedin cattle market here mate," whispered a young rating to me, "the sooner I get back home to my mother the happier I shall be."

"You are lucky," I replied, "I haven't got a mother, perhaps some understanding landlady will take pity on me and mother me for compassion's sake." (I was to find out soon enough!)

My landlady was quite a 'cracker!' Built like Nelson's flagship she bore down on her 'perishing loafers' (as she called her 'guests',) like a 100-gun ship of the line to rake you with her tongue from 'Bowsprit to rudder'

The naval truck shot off. I pressed the doorbell and waited. Eventually, my landlady hove in sight with all sails set to. "Good evening dear lady," (I thought first greetings should always be cordial.)

"Don't give me that load of crap," the 'dear lady' barked! "In the first place I suckled young sods like you when I was in the outback of Australia before you were even born, killed Tiger snakes too with a riding whip as I rode to school, (and that was 30 miles!) Enough of this rabbiting, wipe your feet when you come in! I'll tell you now, I never wanted to act as 'kennel maid' to a load of mixed 'pommy matelots' but there's a bloody war on, I'm forced to take you sods (so the coppers tell me.) For a start I'll have your ration book! I'm a widow, so don't get any funny ideas! My daughter carries a sword everywhere she goes (for her own protection,) you sailors are ruining our girls here in Lowestoft, and another thing, my son-in-law works night and day to make shells for you 'loafers' without men like him, Hitler would walk all over this country!"

She took me to the end of the dining room and pointed… "Can you see anything on the floor?"

"Yes madam, I can see a white line painted across a doorway."

"Good," she barked, "That line is a boundary line, cross it, and you are 'out of bounds' cross it and I 'phone' the

Billeting Officer, cross it, and you leave my house as fast as a bat leaving hell…

"Follow me! Bring your kitbag, 'this is your bed' it's not the 'Ritz' the rooms are crowded, you might find two in a bed at times of emergency billeting. If you are squeamish, you can kip in the bathroom! The last bloke to sleep in your bed was a drunken Scots stoker. He was found in the harbour face down, (I never did like Scots stokers,) as I said to the billeting officer, he should have drowned earlier…

My landlady bade me unpack my gear; wash and scrub, then get downstairs. She relented a little, saying, "You look as if you have wasting disease." Placing a large bowl on the table, along with salt, pepper and vinegar, she insisted that I eat up the mountain of 'cockles' wallowing inside the china basin. "It's sea food," she explained, "As a 'novice' sailor, you need bags of sea food it's only natural! In any event my old man (now departed) had a share in a boat, his 'deckie' supplies me with anything he can catch!"

I thanked her for such a bounty, and a promise of such succulents to come. Then I asked her if she would mind me praying to 'Father Neptune,' and 'Boreas' (God of the North wind) as a tribute to her overwhelming kindness, and her supplier of seafood!

Looking much paler than she had been a few minutes ago, she barked like a four-inch gun, "Not in my bloody dining room you don't, I'm not having any 'Devil dodger or 'Holy Joe' in my establishment. You go and spout in the back garden, not in here!"

Later, in my rock hard bed, I fervently prayed that 'old

Neptune' aided by 'Boreas' would invite nay ensure that my Landladies friend, boat, cockles, winkles and all, would join Neptune down below for an eternal seafood feast!

Night, like a drunken sailor reeled, and all too soon a grey-eyed dawn smiled wearily. Steam, curses and grunts issued from the small bathroom. Tottering in, I tried hard to see the whole expanse of my unshaven face, alas! Competition for the small cracked mirror was (to say the least) fierce. In the end, after scraping another 'Jolly Jacks' face by mistake, I retreated to the bedroom where I completed the shave by looking at my reflection in a boot polish tin lid! The Landlady kicking an old bucket to and fro against an antiquated fire screen heralded breakfast. Porridge, (like glue) piping hot, followed by half a kipper each and a quart of tea to wash it down. Those 'guests' who were late, missed out completely, it was as simple as that.

The journey to the Base only took one hour (if you trotted,) one couldn't get lost, you simply followed hundreds of dark blue coats until you saw scowling sentries standing in gateways and wooden boxes. Often we never made it on time for 'Air raid' warnings would wail and amazingly you could witness the fastest vanishing trick ever devised by man. Behind earth banks, walls, public toilets etc etc. We crouched, or lay as bullets, or shrapnel rattled over the rooftops. Usually, a snow squall, or low cloud signalled that our 'friends' the Luftwaffe were playing cat and mouse with our light and heavy Ante-aircraft fire. A huge blast, a pall of dust smoke and flame told of another 'hit' in this well-known 'Bomb Alley.'

One morning I heard the wail of a diving plane manoeuvring into position near the harbour. Diving into a public toilet, I lay with my mouth open, (chest cushioned on my overcoat,) when the cold marble floor seemed to erupt beneath me. It was the underground blast shockwave. I knew that 'Jerry' had dropped a 'big one.' Suddenly I was showered with urine, cigarette ends and matchsticks as the urinal gully spouted and saturated me in every part. Eyes, mouth, face and body. But, I was 'alive!'

Not far away, amidst girders, bricks, glass and smoke, I saw a priest crying. All around him the mangled bodies of human beings. He turned to me as we scratched away at the rubble and said, "My son, even I doubt that there is a God."

But we carried on, often hoping our 'chit' (drafting) would come up on the walls of our 'Concert Hall Base' (for that was what it was in peace time,) a concert hall, gardens, and Pleasure Park. H.M.S. Europa, (The Sparrows Nest) in peacetime was the Mecca of the minesweeping flotillas, trawlers, (anti-submarine patrol vessels,) and certain light coastal forces! I rubbed shoulders with veteran trawler men, R.N.V.R. (formerly Queens Counsels) and weekend yachtsmen. Royal Naval Reserve members, i.e. Authors, B.B.C. bandsmen etc etc… You name them they could be found 'sculling around' in H.M.S. Europa.

Generally on leaving your 'billet' and arriving at the base, you joined in the fun of a parade, then a dash to get to the canteen. Of course, with age-old Naval tradition, you had a 'duty' to perform. Lectures on gas, and demonstrations on teargas in a bunker to test your gas mask. Sweeping the parade ground, gardening, sentry duty and prisoner escort. They tried very hard to pin you down, 'we' tried very hard to avoid being pinned down! If, by virtue of long usage, or contacts by association, i.e. old shipmates, billet mates, or school chums etc, you could enter the 'magic circle.' This entitled you (via the old pals act) to a cushy number. In effect you became part of the infrastructure, (known as a barrack stanchion.) The Navy became your oyster! You could arrange for a change of billet to a more superior residence in pleasant pastoral surroundings. Transport could be fixed to save your shoe leather! The canteen could be visited, together with the clothing store before or after normal hours... The only rule was this: You never exceeded your privileges, and, you never transgressed the ethical code 'to stick together.' Above all, anyone in the 'magic circle' heard desiring a 'slice of the action at sea' was blackballed and banished forever!

I confess I tried hard to crack it! Mind you, I still scanned the scores of A.F.Os and notices in search of a new course anywhere inland, however, I was unable to find one, you see I had already tried 'em' all!

Then a usually taciturn rating, long in the tooth, cleverly interrogated me as to my 'beliefs and disbeliefs' my concept of duty was closely examined, and my strategy of war. I explained that my strategy was very simple; that when advancing never be first, and when retreating never be last! He smiled ruefully, he was in the same billet as me, very quiet, a 'loner' always well dressed with a well-fed contented look (that I later found out) was the true stamp of a 'magic circle' member. Within twenty-four hours, I saw my name and number on the wall 'chits.' I was ordered to report to the Master-at-Arms for duty as escort to prisoners. All parades, church services or queues a thing of the past! I could travel again on my beloved railways (in reserved carriages) or in taxis to pick up sailors absent without leave.

In effect, we 'happy band of brothers' were employed to 'pick up' anywhere in Britain our unhappy charges who had fouled the nest, and didn't want to return to duty!

We assembled on the concert hall stage (dressed smartly mind,) wearing a bayonet in its scabbard, attached to a shiny leather belt. If, for example any of us got sick and tired of seeing Glasgow by dawn's dreary light in winter, and desired a more pleasant trip to a place near our home or girlfriend, we discussed it like gentlemen after all we had our ethics!

We arranged to share and circulate our journeys so as to increase variety and interest. We believed in democratic discussions and amicable arrangements. We were fanatically loyal to our Master-at-Arms. All he asked for was "Bring 'em' in without trouble and don't over milk the expenses!"

We never let this good man down. Come to think of it our prisoners often had more privileges than those itching to do battle with the enemy! The 'skates' as we fondly called them, only needed to ask to visit the canteen or clothing store etc, and it was done. With the cry "Make way for prisoners and escort" we passed without question through the solid ranks of those queuing up for half an hour. It was always a pleasure to attend to our prisoners needs, and by so doing, we too could circumvent the waiting crowds to get our tea, clothing etc at once!

During an air raid, our prisoners had priority and were released from the cells to go to underground shelters. I often used to think 'there but for the grace of God go any of us'... Reasons for absence or desertion were manifold. Anxiety over families in bombed areas, wife or girlfriend suspected infidelity, evasion of punishment resulting from petty theft or damage etc, or reaching 'breaking point' staying on or over a lawful leave. Booze hangovers, and just plain hatred of the 'service system' and, real or imagined unfair treatment by superiors. Sometimes a strong urge to challenge the Naval machine in its impartial method of turning its members to obey its implacable will. Often, it was just a strong urge for a change of scenery, as simple as that!

It may well be that my 'billet chum' who had skilfully quizzed me with the intensity of an M.15 operative! was influenced by my history of train travel throughout our land by courtesy of the Royal Navy. This quiet recruiter of candidates to the 'magic circle' admitted later that he was of the opinion my travel knowledge of short cuts, even ghost trains and Railway buffets with 'good tea' available, swayed his colleagues in approving my entry to their 'circle.' I deemed it an honour!

Our weekly group 'seminars' freely exchanged ideas to make things easier for our escort parties. Friendly homes en-route, co-operative Station Masters who granted us special reserved compartments on our 'missions of mercy' circulated. Good trains, fast trains, or bloody-minded engines, all were filed away in a massive intelligence network.

We had the right, (by wartime warrant) to insist a stationmaster turn out the occupants of a crowded compartment and place notices on the windows 'Reserved, Prisoner and Escort Naval party.

We could requisition a taxi between rail stations on production of our documents and civil police approval. After all, our prisoners must travel in comfort, and with all haste to meet their punishment!!

The only minor snag was prolonged 'winter excursions' to retrieve our recalcitrants and 'no hopers.' Failing light, when I couldn't view our green and pleasant land was at times trying. Summer journeys were a bonus, and we prayed that more and more of our fellow naval members would desert, (especially if they lived in quiet rural areas!)

Then suddenly, enemy bombing of railways increased. The so-called 'Baedeker' raids on our lovely cathedral cities called for urgent discussions during our weekly seminars. We passed a unanimous motion that we were reaching a 'front line' concept, even the bombers seemed to follow our prisoners and us. It was time to reappraise our position, why; it might even be safer at sea it was suggested!

My friend and fellow 'billet sharer' saw the light! He thought the escort 'agency' he had built up in the barracks was approaching a critical stage. He reasoned that enemy bombers now cut across our lines of communication, in effect 'railway lines' it was (he said) downright uncomfortable, even dangerous not only to us the escorts, but also our prisoners. We had in the past conveyed them without danger, let or hindrance. It has been a matter of professional pride and ethical consideration to conform, chapter and verse to our commitments under the Naval Discipline Act. "The time has come" he went on to fold up our tents and like the Bedouin steal quietly away. "But where to?" I asked.

"My friend," he answered, "I shall now invoke the 'old pals act'."

Within 48hrs, he shook my hand and said, "I'm off to the Isle of Aran, I'm needed there to run a Naval and Church of Scotland library service. The fishing is good (lobsters plentiful) and the only sounds you hear are rutting stags and the call of the cock grouse." This gallant old survivor promised to do all he could to find me a similar 'niche' in the service of our King and Country. As he philosophically remarked, "We have done our bit, let us now steam quietly on in sunlit seas without interruption, our country owes us that." I fervently agreed!

Strangely, the supply of prisoners began to 'dry up!' Was the new intake of naval ratings so bereft of spirit that they were afraid to desert? Or did their parents tell them it would be safer at sea, owing to the widespread attacks on towns and cities! Our Regulating Chief suggested we volunteer to 'opt out' on the basis of 'last in first out.' He of course would have to Officially stand us down. He would of course use his prestige and know how to stream us 'overboard' gently as it were, no member of his elite team would be suddenly drafted to sea, the shock would be far to great! We should all endeavour to avoid such eventualities!

My 'draft' came through the following day; my heart missed a beat when I read that I was being drafted to H.M.S.… Special duties! "Where is she?" I faltered.

"She's a nice little motor cruiser" I was told, she operates on the Suffolk broads, apparently the fishing is first rate too!!

For King and
Country

LANDLADY ON RED ALERT

With heavy hearts and a sense of loss our elite band (escort to prisoners regulating branch) parted company. At once I applied for 3 days compassionate leave (time to adjust to this painful wrench was imperative,) and it is well known that trauma can effect a persons well being, one only has to cite the 1914-1918 war, combat fatigue, shell shock etc. I was sure that I was rapidly becoming another victim! Leave, a change of scenery tranquil repose and good food that was the answer I was certain of it!

Facing my Commander who was now studying my 'request form' I sighed wearily, to my utter surprise he frowned and asked was I not underestimating my request for leave? "It's quite possible Sir," I replied, "but I feel rather guilty in requesting leave when my fellow seamen are being plunged to their watery graves."

"Rubbish," he barked, "guilt doesn't come into it, we all have to die sometime, fact is you are too squeamish, be more assertive man that's an order! The Royal Navy will never tolerate shyness, diffidence, vacillation or hesitation, that sort of thing spreads like a plague throughout a ships company, a ship could be lost as a result! Men are plentiful ships are not! Rephrase your request, look me straight in the eye. Stand up! Speak up! Shut up!" Such an order and from such a senior officer was not to be disregarded, like a 3 inch gun I cracked out,

"Sir! Please amend 3 days to 7 days compassionate leave."

"That's better," he shouted. "Granted! About turn double March." In joyful gratitude I gave him a smart salute saying,
"Thanks awfully sir."

"Not at all young man, continue in your present career and modus operandi and you may well become an officer. Carry on!"

The Regulating Petty Officer standing by his desk screamed, "Get a hair cut! That's an order. Never ever say 'thanks awfully' to an officer, it's conduct unbecoming a seaman of the lower deck! You are not an Etonian just remember that!" Quite frankly I didn't care, for 7 days leave in wartime I would willingly endure the ribald comments of RPOs I would even endure 72hrs in a cage surrounded by the barracks drum and bugle band!

Leave over I returned to my billet, refreshed, rejuvenated and willing to meet the enemy wherever he may be found, praying of course that he wouldn't be found anywhere near me! Due to a re-disposition of manpower I was informed that my 'draft' to my new vessel was to be delayed for a few days, thus I was pressed into duty as a barrack sentry (nights.) Drawing my '1916 vintage Ross 303 rifle and 3 rounds of 'ball ammo MKV1' plus one old belt and bayonet together with gaiters, webbing RN,' I sallied forth! My watch coat (heavy Melton) was rather on the large side, however it did keep me warm from top to toe in those bitter easterly winds. The hem reached my ankles, the collar when turned up covered my hat! Indeed it was difficult (as I was told by a divisional officer) to ascertain whether the coat contained a body or it was a ploy to confuse the foe as to the numerical strength of the guardians of H.M.S. Europa! Frankly I neither knew nor cared what I looked like hiding in my huge 'bell tent of Melton!'

One consideration however was that I had on my guard duty a fellow inmate of my billet, quiet, unassuming, married (quite happily) he hastened to tell me. He hated his naval service and he made a point of showing it in a hundred different ways. You see he was hostilities only called up against his will, he never forgave the naval selection team who thought he would make an excellent cook (his civil job was a bricklayer!) "For the life of me," he implored, "what is the connection?" I gently consoled him by explaining that strange are the ways of service decisions, we never question their infinite wisdom just put our faith in the Almighty and the passage of time. After all, I continued, a dear naval colleague of mine was a trapeze artist and circus acrobat in civil life, but he is now being recommended for a commission in the diplomatic corps!

But I digress, one morning after a particularly savage easterly gale blown snowstorm my friend and I wearily returned to our billet, hungry, bitterly cold, fingers feet and even eyelashes frozen together. It was still quite early, steam covered the windows and we tiptoed up the garden path to the back door. Silently we entered and as we did so the most tantalising aroma assailed our nostrils. Sharpened by the pangs of hunger we crossed the dreaded white boundary line (out of bounds to all naval ratings) and taking care to discard our boots in 'neutral territory' we crept like cat burglars to the sanctum sanctorium, or to be more specific we entered the kitchen and its oven!

Opening the oven door we gasped in admiration and mounting excitement! Succulent rosy rashers of bacon lay in all their glory being cuddled be a quartet of eggs, eggs plump with great yolks like the rising sun on a winter's day. I whispered to Frank, "My God, free range too, do you think the landlady has cooked these for us? perhaps she has had a twinge of conscience."

"More like a brainstorm," muttered Frank! We shovelled the piping hot feast down our gullets like pelicans on a picnic! Carefully replacing the dinner plate we crept upstairs past the snoring bodies and sank into our own respective beds, eyes glazed, faces aglow, teeth cleaned and then oblivion!

Suddenly all hell broke loose! I awoke to a wailing and shrieking in my eardrum. "Out! Out! Get Out!" feet thundered from every room and down the stairs.

"It's an air raid," I shouted to Frank, "quick, grab your

helmet and gas mask." Downstairs we were mustered in the dining room, our female 'Dracula' eyes blazing, supported by her daughter and son-in-law came to the point. "Thieves! Thieves! The lot of you open your mouths wide." She closely examined our teeth rather like a woodpecker peering under the bark of a tree. "My son-in-law has just come off night shift making shells for the likes of you lot you thieving bastards," she shrieked and someone has stolen his breakfast! "I'll look in every mouth in the place and if I find crumbs, egg yolk, or bacon bits whoever's responsible it's curtains for 'em,' you treacherous thieving sods so help me God, I'll flay you alive and feed you to the mackerel."

Mind you, I had to admire this determined woman, anyone willing to peer into the gaping jaws of boozy stokers and seamen is truly heroic, nay downright suicidal, even at a distance this motley collection of sleepy sea dogs belched and wagged their disgusting coated tongues as they ruefully leered with bloodshot eyes at old 'Mother Shipton.' I whispered to Frank, "Christ I wonder if they know they have halitosis?"

Believing as I did in peace, conciliation and avoidance of 'scenes' especially inflammatory ones I decided to defuse the situation, after all if old 'Nestor' could pacify the sulking Achilles in his tent then surely I could de-acidify this rapidly boiling and bubbling landlady! "Dear Madam, allow me to suggest that anger never did promote wise counsel, after all we have all suffered in one way or another, I myself for instance still have not had my own breakfast after a bitterly cold spell of sentry duty" (this was said to create a belief in my own innocence in the mind of 'madam') the situation was becoming critical!

It seemed to me that the anger of this 'Boadicea of the Billets' would equal indeed even surpass the anger of Achilles who according to Homer in his delightful epic 'the Iliad' fulminated throughout the length of that poem! Once again I pleaded for tolerance and understanding saying, "After all are we not all your chickens (appealing to her maternal instinct) you are 'ipso facto in 'loco parentis'."

"That's just about all I'm going to take from you, you bloody foreigner," she rasped. "I've always had my doubts about you, you oily would be parson in a con-man's jacket, it's to the billeting officer I go you load of work-shy, thieving carrion crows."

Well at least she had hoisted her battle pennant we knew where we stood now all right. "Thanks a bunch mate," muttered Frank in my direction.

For King and Country

DEFENCE OF THE REALM

Within 24 hours of my Landlady declaring 'unrestricted warfare' on her 'guests' I abandoned ship! He who fights then runs away lives to fight another day! To my mind simple maxims are best, indeed as my old granny used to say, "If you cannot advance one yard, don't move, mark time its called marching without moving!" I abhor confrontation or violence, not for me fisticuffs or rough brawling, I much prefer pistols at dawn or swords even, so much more gentlemanly I always think! However, as a tactical preference on the field of battle I would recommend the following: – When advancing never be first but when retreating never be last!

My 'draft chit' awaited me at the barracks. I was to proceed with all dispatch to HMS Blank.

"Could I have my travel warrant Chief," I asked the drafting master.

"No lad not this time, I know how you love 'chuff chuffs' but this time it's a five penny bus ride, in your case however grab the provision truck in 30 minutes 'chop chop'."

The thought occurred to me that as I was proceeding 'on draft' I could demand a meal bag just as if my journey was to Scapa Flow and beyond! So to the Naafi Canteen I marched and presented my draft chit, the assistant frowned, "HMS…? Where is she?" Invoking security in wartime I answered,

"Classified, most secret and confidential." This must have been impressive for after a wait of only 10 minutes he handed me the well known 'meal bag,' usually even on journeys of several hundred miles or more the stock fare was: – 2 rock cakes (well named) 1 apple (often a cooker) 1 cheese sandwich, or a spam/fish paste filling.

To this very day, I shall never find out who the joker was who filled my bag for it contained the following:- 6 cheese sandwiches, 3 apples (coxes) 6 apple tarts, 6 barley sugar sweets, 1 bar of chocolate and 1 dozen matches (in tinfoil.) The only thing lacking was a compass, pistol with 5 rounds of 'ammo' a fishing line and a map of German submarine pens! It was obvious that the Naafi staff knew more about H.M.S. 'Blank' than I did. Most surprising of all was the fact that she was berthed only 2 miles away, and all that food was given to me for such a short journey to 'Oulton Broads.'

Soon I reached my destination and reported to the duty coxswain, I remarked on my voluptuous meal bag for such a short journey? "Let not your conscience trouble you," he smiled, "we work in mysterious circles here, the Naafi manager in the barracks is a good customer of ours, he gives his personal attention to all who are sent here it's a sort of 'quid-pro-quo' you understand?"

"Yes Coxswain," I replied, "but my education is rather limited so do I take it that you mean perhaps 'pare-passu?'"

"Welcome aboard," he said shaking my hand. "I really do believe that you understand after all."

Later I was introduced to my 'shipmates.' Never have I seen such a diverse and motley collection of sea dogs in our northern hemisphere! To crew H.M.S....? We had a brace of Coxswains, 1 Telegraphist, 2 Engineers 4 Seamen. The Base staff were also well represented consisting of: – 1 Lieutenant (R.N.V.R) 1 Clerk, 1 Cook, 1 Steward and 1 Sick Berth Attendant (better known as a poultice walloper.) In fact the majority of the complement were R.N.V.R.. It used to be held that Royal Naval Officers were gentlemen not sailors, and R.N.V.R. were sailors and not gentlemen, but Royal Naval Volunteer Reserve Officers were neither sailors nor gentlemen! Personally speaking I cannot fully subscribe to that dictum.

Our Lieutenant (R.N.V.R.) may not be quite termed a 'gentleman' or even a sailor, but by God he was an excellent angler specialising in Bream and Pike in the very river we were 'resting' in! One Coxswain was a fine sailor familiar with Cowes Week etc., the other one hated water of any sort! He was an old Etonian of course! One seaman was a wild fowler in Blakeney on the east coast, and another was a poacher, whilst our Telegraphist was the son of a bishop and the Cook was a former chef with an unsavoury reputation but he could create a meal from sea boot stockings or the odd oily cormorant that dared to come within range. Our Clerk aspired to greatness by virtue of promotion to leading writer, whilst our Steward looked forward to seducing any female within his grasp, and last but not least our Sick Bay Wallah (a qualified vet) R.N.V.R. played a violin and smoked cigars! It was our 'vet' who asked me what my profession was? To which I replied, "quite frankly I haven't made my mind up yet, in fact I'm not quite sure what I am!" He stared hard and then rapidly departed to his cabin.

Later on I was briefed by the coxswains. "Doubtless," said the Etonian, "you are wondering what we do here, it really is quite straightforward, we are a reserve special group and it's strictly hush-hush, our privileges are commensurate with the nature of our task, namely to lie low until we are required. If the enemy shoot at us we shoot back do you understand?"

"Quite so coxswain, after all it seems a reasonable thing to do."

"Splendid," said the Etonian, "we are here primarily to defend our country, any questions?"

"Yes Sir, what do we defend our country with?"

"Jolly good question," he replied. "The answer is simple, 3 Ross rifles and bayonets and 1 Vickers .5 machine gun to be used only if the enemy shoot first, we are not an offensive force, we are a clandestine unit trained never to show ourselves or invite aggressive action! Of course should there ever be any shooting it will be you that will have the honour to return fire, after all you are a trained gunnery fellow so do you understand the orders?"

"Perfectly Coxswain," I replied. "I only shoot if they shoot first seems quite logical even sensible to me."

"Well said guns, that's the spirit I think we can enjoy our time in the Royal Navy, thank God we see eye to eye so far, oh, and by the way, do you fish?"

"Most certainly Sir."

"And do you shoot pheasants, mallard, partridge and pigeons?"

"Of course Sir."

"Good, we shall sally forth at sunset, the fowl will be in by then and we shall be visiting the pike lines. Bream are plentiful too, one hand grenade and we can send a consignment up to Billingsgate market on the night train!"

The yachting coxswain invited me to familiarise myself with our ship, her vital statistics as he put it. He described her performance and waxed eloquent on her 'co-efficient of fineness and turning circle etc., "You see guns," he ensued, "She is no ordinary craft she was owned by a millionaire who is now a Cabinet Minister who insists we report on her progress every month! We run her on high octane fuel (the stuff our spitfires drink,) we can knock 25 knots out of her with a wind astern, however, in deference to the Minister's plea not to strain her but run her as often as possible in 'fresh water' we paddle along at 5 knots on the river. This serves to prevent damage to the banks and enables us to view the numerous flora and fauna of our lovely Suffolk Broads."

"Most commendable," I murmured, "we must resist pressure to strain her at sea!"

"Precisely," he said. "As a low profile group we are committed to avoid any unpleasantness with German E.Boats, R.Boats, or Dive Bombers. We never attract adverse comment i.e racing up and down the 'fairway' or estuary like these newly commissioned destroyers 'showing off,' however, unfortunately we must put to sea at least once a month."

My heart missed a beat! "Is that really necessary Coxswain?" I asked.

"Afraid so," he answered, "mind you this is a condition imposed by 'Customs' and Naval Regulations to enable us to qualify for 'duty free' tobacco and cigarettes (H.M. Ships only) At sixpence for 20 Senior Service it's worth the risk!"

We creep down river under the bridge and enter the harbour mouth, of course we are dressed in our best white polo neck sweaters issued to light coastal forces! It's rather touching really, the crews of minesweepers, corvettes, even the odd destroyer! They man the rails and cheer us on with great feeling, we dip our ensign in return! It's quite possible they think we are a submarine crew recuperating from an attack on the 'Tirpitz' such is the brotherhood of the Royal Navy! We cruise to our favourite sand spit then as dusk falls we slip our small beam trawl net astern. Codling, dabs and 'flatties' are all a welcome addition to our naval rations, any surplus are exchanged for fresh fruit and vegetables from our friendly farmers! Having put in our 24hrs stint at sea we return refreshed with cartons of cigarettes and perhaps a spare jar of neat rum from our supply contacts!

The quarters allocated to us were to say the least so different from the usual 'Naval Shore Establishments!' A large boathouse well thatched, warm in winter and cool in summer was our home from home, five yards from the riverside berth and our vessel. We slept on canvas trestle beds, and due to our sporting members' 'thoughtfulness' gleaming polished shotguns festooned the walls. Long nets for capture of rabbits, gate nets, snares, fishing nets, keep nets, and landing nets. Beam trawl nets (2 of them) lay discreetly on a shelf above the gun racks. Behind the meat safe (covered by ships canvas) frolicked and scratched half a dozen polecat ferrets in their hutch, adjacent to the cook's kitchen was a large box, in it was old tealeaves, damp hessian sacking and newspaper. On opening the lid one could see the greatest collection of plump maggots and various larvae, in the other compartment were the finest red, juicy earthworms this side of Christendom!

It was obvious that I was now in situ with the 'crème-de-la-crème' of poachers, deep-sea trawlermen, coarse fish experts, and shooting fanatics! I knew then that if the 'hour of danger' should approach England my 'Shipmates' would survive come what may and I intended to be with them! The time came and I was taught to 'bab' for eels harpoon them or take them in willow wand traps, also, to take a pheasant silently, braid nets of every type, snare pike and fat rabbits and ferret the warrens on the river banks. "We are doing the River Board a service," it was explained. I enjoyed shooting parties in back waters, stubble and marsh, and angled for Roach, Bream and Perch etc,

We, the Royal Navy had (it appeared) jurisdiction on the waterways to maintain the anti-plane and boat obstructions across the 'Broads.' The spiked booms could be quite a problem even to us! The Army Artillery controlled the landward sides, Guns (hidden by netting) covered the area, but we had an arrangement with Battery Commanders to inform them in advance when we cruised up the river by night to thin out the fish and game. We had a 'gentlemen's agreement' to share the 'spoils' and a barter system, which worked splendidly!

The routine was simple. Breakfast ample and sufficient, then a mini parade. Our Lieutenant (R.N.V.R.) was a native of the area, he lived but a short distance away thus he was home every night, returning in the morning to 'Inspect, 'peruse signals,' receive request-men or issue new orders. He fished as often as he could and was a 'match angler' quick, dextrous, he rarely failed to catch his quarry, he 'read' the water very well and cursed the interruption to his concentration when enemy bombers skimmed over us especially during rain squalls or misty weather. Thus for the reasons mentioned above we had the nights to ourselves generally. Serious incidents of course reached him and he would return to take over command. As far as possible we or rather our Coxswains avoided calling him out unless absolutely necessary.

Late one night, our valiant telegraphist (and son of a bishop) came into our blacked out quarters. "Chaps," he said, "its just come over the R.T. Set that Great Yarmouth is copping it, jerry is out in force."

"That means he will plaster Lowestoft next," said the coxswain. "The moon is full but plenty of scudding cloud about, which means one thing, we can take a few roosting pheasants. Lord…. up the river will be taking cover (I'll see to that) I shall warn the army too they will be 'on edge' and may be trigger happy, I have no desire to be shot by a bloody squaddie! The estate old retainers will go to ground like old dog foxes! Lowestoft's sky will be well lit up with searchlights and flares, and the noise will be just right to disguise our shots!"

By 22:00hrs we had crept up the river, faces blackened and .410 guns with half charge cartridges at the ready. We moored up alongside a spinney large and full of plump birds, as our Leading Seaman remarked too many old cock birds will do no good, we are doing his Lordship a favour by culling them!

By 2:00 a.m. we rendezvoused with the army jeep alongside the river and 15 birds were handed over plus a carton of cigarettes.

We returned to our base with 22 plump pheasants, then washing our dainty launch down well, we entered in the log, "Anti-magnetic (parachute) mine patrol carried out. Heavy fire over Lowestoft, nothing to report. All in order!

For King and
Country

~&~

THE SHOOTING PARTY

Christmas drew near. I awoke to see large snowflakes like barn owls feathers falling slowly, softly, silently to clothe roads, roofs and exposed land. Trees and shrubs looked especially beautiful covered in a mantle of sparkling crystals. Christmas, a time of peace, goodwill and sentimental childhood memories. Such a time or scene I mused inspired great poets like Milton to write: – Ode on the morning of Christ's Nativity. Who now I wondered will at this point in time write an ode to war and violence, an ode to the dreadful preparations for Death throughout our Nation?

Suddenly a cry echoed around our boathouse base, "Clear lower decks." Our Lieutenant appeared turned about and then left us!

Clear lower decks meant only one thing, an assembly or muster of Naval personnel to await (generally speaking) the 'weighing off' for punishment or acquittal of a fellow seaman, or, the command to 'keep silence' and gather to await important news from an officer so appointed.

We stared uncomfortable and suspicious at each other, who had betrayed? "Was it I coxswain?" I murmured.

"Was it me?" said his fellow coxswain.

"Fall in on the mess deck," sung out our coxswain, "keep silence now, stand easy."

"Thank you coxswain," spoke our Lieutenant, "listen carefully now this is most important, secret, and urgent!" My God, I thought we are to be sent on a dangerous mission at last, what a time to order us into action, and nigh on Christmas too! I wondered whether by coming to this 'outfit' I had been the victim of a malicious Master-at-Arms who knew more than I did. The thought of a perilous journey down through the harbour, and perhaps skirting the Scrobie Sands filled me with dread.

"You look quite pale 'Guns'," said our lieutenant, "do you feel fit enough?"

"It's the snows reflection sir," I faltered, "I'm perfectly all right sir."

"You had better be," he answered, "shortly you will be taking part in a hard day's shooting (no not at the enemy!) but you will attend us as 'loader' to our guests during a 'grand slam!' at game and waterfowl! It's a pre-Christmas shooting party 'guns,' so let us pray that 'Jerry' attacks Yarmouth instead of Lowestoft! Now pay attention chaps" he continued, "for sometime past I have been involved (unknown to you) in a different logistical exercise. This is the burden I bear as a Naval Officer, so Christ help you if you let me down! Why even now as I speak a destroyer is unloading a consignment of prime Scottish salmon in Lowestoft harbour, she has rushed down from the Western Approaches (Scotland) by order of the Admiral Commanding. Our own cook by now will be supervising the unloading for reception here at our base. This salmon will form part of a picnic lunch on Thursday (the day of the shoot.) Our guests should I hope do justice to our cook's efforts, he tells me that roast pork, boiled ham and smoked salmon should tempt our guests' appetites. Fine old whisky (20 years in the 'still') will hasten their appreciation of our preparations! Beaters, (culled from the local Artillery Battery) will receive beetroot and cheese sandwiches plus one bottle of cordial, after all we don't want these squaddies 'paralytic' from stronger beverages, sober beaters means efficient flushing of pheasants! …

The guests are as follows: – The owner of the cabin cruiser we currently use 'Sir Robert…? (Minister of production) will be accompanied by the Sea Lord, both I may add were at Eton College with the father of our present Coxswain, who himself attended that illustrious college! I'm sure you will make them feel at home!

"As a tribute to the Royal Artillery, 6 Battery Commanders are invited after they co-operate with us in every way especially when guarding the approaches to our river, and the fish and fowl you doubtless know exist therein? The Destroyer Captain who kindly rushed our salmon down from a Scottish loch is also on the guest list! Our own 'supremo' from the base is to be with us, hc is a very dependable shot, who specialises in bringing down fast old cock birds curling down wind, but much more important his presence on such an occasion will ensure that we remain here! Depend upon it, if we omit to invite our Supremo and by all the Admirals in heaven we shall be in Hong Kong by the New Year!

"In conclusion gentlemen," he waxed eloquent, "you in the launch will rendezvous above the town bridge at 0:900hrs sharp! Three trot boats will form up in line, guests will be dressed in Naval duffel coats with a fine silk tassel around the waist. The object is to ensure that any 'prying eyes' on each side of the bank will think our guests are a party of 'Benedictine Monks' visiting some holy shrine or other!

"Cruising quietly at 5 knots, proceed to the estate landing stage steps for disembarkation, bodyguards and beaters will be ready. His Lordship will also be in position having been conveyed in his palanquin by sturdy foresters, that is all, carry on coxswain, 'pipe up spirits'." (a most welcome sound to all seamen as it signifies a tot of 'Nelson's Blood.')

The shoot was enjoyed by guests and loaders alike, however the 'beaters' mud caked, scratched and wet through complained bitterly! Our 'guns' (tanked up with fine 'glen livet') brought down pheasant, partridge, snipe and woodcock.

'Miscellaneous' targets included one old flea bitten tomcat, 10 magpies and several carrion crows. The Sea Lord 'winged' a brace of beaters at 50 yards range and remarked that they were too slow, too lazy and too incompetent! "After all," he said, "by straying out of line they had prevented his usual classic 'left and right' victory over a brace of woodcock!"

As I was loader to the Sea Lord I commented on the unusual absence of enemy aircraft activity, I even postulated my belief that if we fired no shots, nor did the enemy life would be much more pleasant!"

"Rubbish," was his reply, "someone has to open the batting, how can anyone win or lose a war unless someone shoots at the other? We British would never win a war if both sides just blew kisses at one another!" He did concede however that we had organised a first rate days sport in a dangerous area of repeated enemy activity, was in itself a mark of the Royal Navy's adaptation to any given situation! Thus, he would recommend a few days leave for all of us. Our Lieutenant would be recommended for a D.S.C. to mark his unstinting efforts to ensure his operation was a success. Permission was also given to the loaders to retain anything left over in the picnic hamper. The beaters (army) were allowed to take – two dozen wood pigeon and 6 moorhens for their own use.

"A most generous gift," said their C.O. Battery Commander Royal Artillery!

For King and Country

INVASION – FINIS

I have often been asked this question: What was the most interesting episode during your time on naval service?

Invariably my reply is – the time we believed that the enemy had arrived! It was like this: – As we reclined in our comfortable mess deck a peacetime thatched boat house on the banks of the river Waveney Oulton Broad, our telegraphist rushed in pale and trembling, "Coxswain," he spluttered, "This is it! This is it!"

"WHAT precisely is it Sparks? Pull yourself together man one would think that the bloody invasion had started!"

"It has Coxswain, my God it has! I have just left our vessel (I was coming off watch on R.T. Duty when the code word flashed through. 'To all Forces, Imminent Invasion, sea borne forces sighted operate your procedural response'! Radio silence in force 'NOW' over and out!')

Praise be to God for this most glorious hour! Once more into the breech dear sea dogs! 'Let us fill up our vessel with plenty of bread' I chanted, (hoping 'Rupert Brooke' and 'Shakespeare' would forgive my imitation!!

"Christ," said the Coxswain, 'Jerry' would drop in just as our old man (the Lieutenant) has gone to Liverpool to visit his parents! Right! Everyone prepare to carry out the procedure. Load our craft with everything movable and usable – Shotguns, Rods, Nets, even the Ferrets! The enemy must not get his hands on our stuff! Ammunition, Beef Cheese, Blankets, Medical kit, Spare tools, (not to mention every rum jar!) Oh and then get over to Robinson's slipway and fill her up with 100 octane juice (we may have to exceed our usual 5 knots! Camouflage netting. Everything, repeat Everything that we can stow aboard for our survival – See to it at the double!"

Thus we sprung into action! Quickly we loaded our launch with as much as we could to ensure our ultimate survival. Never did I witness such a concerted unity of purpose. Silently we beavered away and finally we shot across to Robinson's slipway to fuel up our now 'filled to capacity' motor launch.

This sudden and unheralded 'call to arms' was to say the least a nuisance! No notice of intent was given to our chaps? As our Etonian Coxswain said, "after all one doesn't send a telegram to the 'other side' with the E.T.A. on it we are not playing rugby at twickers you know, of course we had ample warning!

Our 'Periclean Prime Minister' with his sonorous and serious tones had invoked our National pride, an age-old resistance to tyranny, each of us would fight on (he of course in his bomb shelter!!) We would Never! Never! Surrender! As I remarked to my fellow seaman: – "If proud France is now lying prostrate under the German jackboot, we must realise that our native land is now the only barrier to the Nazi dream of World Domination and Conquest. We must repel this monstrous and evil Nazi madman lest we sink under the weight of a barbaric and pitiless war machine."

"That's enough of that 'Guns'," my Coxswain barked, such platitudes and oratorical dissertations are best left to Politicians and 'Bible Thumpers' not seamen on half a crown a day! Fine words don't win wars," he concluded.

All these discursive efforts took place as we tanked up with fuel. Our 'yachting Coxswain' invoked that well known service ploy 'Seniority.' "It seems to me," he said, "that in the absence of our Lieutenant, I as 'senior rating' will assume command, Agreed?" We were more than happy to agree of course! He thanked us for our support saying, "I will simplify matters, our 'rules of engagement' are perfectly clear, we have been instructed to avoid damage to this valuable vessel at all costs, 'Agreed'?" We agreed unanimously! "In that case," he went on, we proceed at once up river in the direction of Beccles to begin with." We needed no further orders and thanked God that we had such a sensible coxswain in charge!

Fuelling completed we prepared to leave. "Permission to take the wheel Coxswain?" I sang out.

"Certainly not 'Guns' by God no, you may have

taken everything else but the wheel NEVER! The second coxswain will take the wheel." Our (now very anxious to leave) Etonian sung out,

"It's a pleasure, 260 degrees magnetic is it?"

"NO' was the answer, creep up to the starboard bank, follow it very closely, quietly, and slowly, we must not create any panic or alarm amongst the occupants of adjoining properties. We shall set an example of calmness thus allaying any hysteria due to unfounded rumour. 'Guns' to the bow of the vessel, lie flat with a boat hook at the ready, if we 'yaw' into the bank you will be required to fend us off."

"Then I can't mount my .5 Vickers gun '*coxswain*' protested.

"'NO' you cannot, that's an order! Remember, we are a low profile unit, to fire even one round would cause much alarm, and this would jeopardise all my plans to avoid confrontation. My primary duty is to lead our vessel and her crew away from needless hostility, now, man the boat hook, quietly I say even as I speak advance units of German Paratroops may be approaching us via the river footpaths! Camouflage our structure, don your balaclavas, No smoking. Periodic heaving to alongside and under the bank will be carried out. Listen out for enemy activity and pay attention to wildfowl disturbance, wood pigeon and lapwings are good indicators of human intrusion, so are cattle. It's a full moon, treat with caution farm animals seen congregating and staring in the direction of a spinney or hedgerow."

"Supposing Coxswain," I whispered, "our friends the army patrols think that we are the German Special Service

Units coming inland? Let's face it Coxswain, it would be a crying shame to be shot by our own soldiers, British bullets in British rifles," I protested.

"All right 'Guns' no need to panic, the last thing I did before coming aboard was to warn the Army Commander that we were coming up river to assist him in defence!"

"What did he say?" asked the Telegraphist. The reply was,

"That's what I was afraid of!"

I was relieved at the bow of the vessel by the Leading Seaman himself a professional wild fowler in peacetime. His home was not too far away in Wells-next-the-sea. "Nothing doing as yet," I said handing him the boat hook.

"Could be a false alarm you know," he gestured towards the east, no flares, no shots quiet as a grave, isn't it? Probably our blokes are letting 'em' filter in to the jaws of the trap then that's their lot, 'eh'."

"More like our bloody lot mate," I replied, "too quiet for my liking!"

"Better go aft for your cocoa and chicken leg, it's a scratch meal, cookie says he's not allowed to use his stove too risky, incidentally have you made a will out yet? I have!"

Leaving this prophet of doom I slithered like a Dover sole across the deck to the cabin 'aft.'

So off we glided leaving Lowestoft and our Base at Oulton Broad astern. The tall reeds gravely bowed and bobbed as we left them behind. They seemed to whisper a message in the soft night air that only they and the creatures they sheltered could understand. I wondered how many voles, moorhens, warblers, foraging foxes, or stoats even perhaps a rare bittern were watching us as we slid by? The Coxswain said, "half over, stop engines, prepare to make fast!" We entered an arching tunnel of willow, alder, and blackthorn scrub, a natural concealed backwater (apparently well known to our coxswain) this was to be our billet for the time being 'Watches set,' the remainder went to 'diving stations' (bed)

Dawn and the scene was one of tranquillity, not a bird or beast advertised alarm signalling unusual human activity. Rooks flew in massed legions of black tumbling bodies as they sported and crossed to marshland and meadow. Jackdaws clacked and gossiped overhead. Mallard, Redshank, and Curlew quacked, whistled and bubbled on mudflat and lagoon. "Seems all right to me," said our cook itching to fry up and eat up.

"We'll wait for our 'scouts' first," ordered the Coxswain, "if they don't come back then we lie low." Soon our 'poacher' and his number two the wild fowler appeared. A brace of Rhode Island Red Chickens also turned up!

"Nothing to report Coxswain," they remarked, "everything appears normal, these chickens were so surprised at strangers near their hen house they collapsed in our arms!"

"Good lads," said the coxswain, "hands to breakfast!"

Breakfast over, a 'Council of Captains' was called by our Coxswain. "So far so good, but we must act with caution. No rubbish or human waste will be chucked overboard, potential enemy forces down river would soon see it and realise that service or civilian personnel were, or had been upriver recently. Bury it, we must be constantly on guard to avert an ambush, 'Guns' when your turn comes up to be a scout, you will move like a phantom, any questions?"

"Yes Coxswain, what if I am captured alive? What am I supposed to do?"

"That's easy 'Guns,' to avoid interrogation and possible divulging of our location you will feign insanity, which should not prove too difficult for you! They will probably think that you are 'bomb happy' (and they would probably be right.) I often think 'Guns' that you are one of natures casualties."

The Leading Seaman and I explored the area adjacent to our now netted and camouflaged backwater. To our great surprise not too far from us in a bend in the river we found a long, low, rambling building, which turned out to be a riverside pub, complete with its own jetty, boathouse, and orchard. We doubled back to our vessel and on describing this utopian dwelling convinced our Coxswain that this was worth a further inspection, 'Reconnaissance by night!' Our poaching and wild fowling 'duo' crept forth. Reporting back later 'No Dogs,' occupants two (husband and wife,) Publican and Barmaid in the summer, odd jobbing in the winter months. Suffolk born and bred, have no knowledge of invasion! Generous people, (they gave us a tot) and suggest we move into the Boathouse as invited guests, (non-paying of course!) No other persons frequent their patch due to wartime ban on non-essential civilians in a designated garrison area. Nearest village Burgh-St-Peter, occasional visits made to that village by garrison troops inspecting mined area and observation points. "Splendid," said our coxswain, "we move house tomorrow night after I have inspected the area personally. If the weather remains dry and sunny we shall enjoy home comforts, rest, and well-deserved recreation! After all, too long in our vessel is bound to create feelings of frustration and an insidious restriction of our liberty!"

The move to our 'new abode' passed without incident, the only member of our crew unable to assist was our steward. Due to our sudden departure by reason of our 'imminent invasion' alarm he had been left behind, doubtless scrutinising the 'behind' of his latest female paramour in some remote village, his sexual appetite knew no bounds, as the coxswain remarked, "I would not trust him with a sniff at a barmaid's apron, let us hope that he is now surrounded by enemy paratroops prodding his behind with bayonets!"

"Speaking of paratroops," said our telegraphist, "suppose they don't arrive in and around Lowestoft and in fact Great Yarmouth is their destination? Even now they may be advancing in a wide arc to encircle us eventually, in other words are we doing the right thing staying here? It's very worrying you know."

"Of course it is 'Sparks'," replied the coxswain, "we don't know which way they are heading, but then they don't know which way WE are heading, agreed? They won't tell us their destination, thus we don't tell them ours, it's only fair after all isn't it?"

Up piped coxswain number two,(Etonian.) "Quite so it is logical to assume their 'Modus operandi' is merely commensurate with Our 'Modus operandi' they cannot complain if we operate at all times within the concept of 'quid-pro-qua' eh chaps." The yachting coxswain understood this philosophic discourse, after all he had had a Grammar School education, "Well said," he remarked. Our poacher too threw in his 'bunch of fives' saying,

"What you really mean is that if 'jerry' doesn't tell us everything, we won't tell him right?"

"Right!" said the Etonian.

"Right!" We all echoed.

"In any case our plan is simple, imaginative and bold," replied the Coxswain, "If 'Jerry' turns right we turn left, when he rests we rest, if he should turn this way we turn the other way! We know every channel, watercourse, and ditch. If he seeks us we will hide, after all it is in our interest that he never finds us, better still that he never even sees us! Or we him!" We all applauded our Coxswain's tactical skill and appreciation of our situation, we decided to be behind him all the way, 'well behind him!'

We ate, 'cleaned ship,' and discreetly extended our area of search, (not for the enemy of course) this would have been wilful disobedience of our Coxswain's orders! To avoid any unpleasantness 'i.e. confronting the other side' we searched only for fish, fowl, and as easy a life as possible, not much to ask for surely?

This utopian ideal had its limitations however, pragmatism and practicality put paid to all that. No 'action' became discernible, no pay parade made one miserable! A strange, unreal aspect of our existence manifested itself!

The turning point came quite suddenly, the Army turned us in! (The British Army I hasten to add, not the 'other army')

Our 'poaching' Leading Seaman could contain himself no longer. He spotted a fine old ring necked cock pheasant standing on a gatepost some 200 yards away, alas, old habits die hard and seizing a 303 service rifle (forgetful of orders not to attract the enemy's attention by shooting) he knocked his victim a few yards downwind. Unfortunately, his line of 'sight' included a very fine farmhouse some 800 yards distance! Off flew some tiles, and up sprang the farmer's wife to upbraid the local garrison Commander by telephone. She put in a claim for compensation saying, "This is not, repeat not, a bloody shooting range!"

The military Jeep with its 'posse' of red-faced 'red caps' with binoculars homed in. By this time our sharpshooter had taken cover on seeing them approach, he at once surmised by their method of approach that in effect he (and us!) the boat and all it contained were (to quote that old naval saying) 'Adrift!'

I suppose all things must end, and we prepared to leave. We decided on a night departure as good men-of-war ships often do. Like condemned prisoners we ate heartily. Our 'host' the publican regretted our proposed journey, he personally wished we could have been his 'guests' till the end of hostilities. To placate his evidently sincere feelings, we sold him a jar of neat rum (navy for the use of) at a discount price, he promised never to tell a soul. Our Etonian called him a jolly decent chap and British through and through!

The night was bible black, without stars, moon or lonely cry of curlew, red shank or widgeon. We slipped our moorings to glide stealthily down river, destination our Base and to meet our superiors. Quietly we glided with barely a chuckle from engine or propeller. Looking at his watch our Coxswain said in a low voice grave as the Lord Chief Justice, "Steady as she goes, keep a sharp bow lookout not far to go now!"

Suddenly our launch lurched scraping her keel and tilting to port. "STOP ENGINES!" The water gurgled around us, bilges and compartments remained dry. "Half astern" then "Full astern" was the order. She groaned, rumbled, and shuddered but to no avail, we had run aground! Eventually, dawn pale, wan and cold emerged to show us the reason for this unfortunate accident. Quite simply, a large portion of the riverbank with its shrubs and nettles etc. had given way. Our boat resembled a partially submerged 'hippo' resting in an African river...

Our 'friends' the local army contingent soon spotted us from their 'pillboxes' and observation posts on high ground above us. Still smarting from the 'whiplash tongue' of the farmer's wife (she of the lost tiles) they, thirsting for blood informed our base at once. We were placed in 'open arrest' and conveyed to 'Caesar's palace!' "Thank God," said our telegraphist, "we are not to be put in the gladiators arena or the lion pit."

The verdict of the Naval Court was unanimous, we, each and every one of us wholeheartedly agreed with the findings as follows...

The accused, on the evidence before us cannot safely be found guilty as charged.

Conditions at the time were fluid, uncertain and indecisive. In the absence of their commanding officer, himself on lawful leave, the Coxswains of the said ship-of-war by virtue of dire emergency assumed command. They followed the 'Invasion Imminent' standing orders and maintained radio silence. It has been questioned as to the 'tactical wisdom' of proceeding west (inland) instead of east to the suspected enemy approach, however, bearing in mind the general uncertainty of the whole sequence of events, we believe their decision was a wise one...

My Lords of Admiralty will support any reasonable decision made by the officer of the watch or substitute as in this case. Indecision will 'never be tolerated.' As to the shooting of a cock pheasant with a service rifle contrary to Fleet Gunnery Orders, we cannot substantiate such a charge. The only witnesses were army patrols whose evidence we have noted in the past were suspect, flawed, and often actuated by jealousy.

Thus the accused will leave this court without a stain on their hitherto unimpeachable characters. We wish them well in their chosen careers. They are to be highly commended for their devotion to duty and the highest traditions of the Royal Navy!

Such a vindication, indeed praise from a panel of such distinguished Naval Officers was a sweet and heady wine. Meeting in a tavern later we solemnly toasted the presiding officers in fine old vintage port. Our bond of comradeship was even more forged by our will to 'swing together.'

Our yachting coxswain was promoted to Chief Petty Officer, with 14 days special leave for his presence of mind in difficult circumstances! Our Etonian coxswain a commission to Sub. Lt. R.N.V.R. and drafted to St Ives Cornwall. He was to liase with the Crown Film Unit on propaganda and morale boosting films, 'The Bulldog Barks' etc. The remainder of that happy band of brothers were retained pending orders. As the Commodore of the Base said, "I can ill afford to lose such men!"

The ship? She was de-commissioned, and taken by Naval long loader to her home berth at Teddington Lock, River Thames to be reunited with her owner the Cabinet Minister...

FINIS